A Life Reimagined

A Life Reimagined

*My Journey of Hope
in the Midst of Loss*

JILL HALFPENNY

MACMILLAN

First published 2024 by Macmillan
an imprint of Pan Macmillan
The Smithson, 6 Briset Street, London EC1M 5NR
EU representative: Macmillan Publishers Ireland Ltd, 1st Floor,
The Liffey Trust Centre, 117–126 Sheriff Street Upper,
Dublin 1, D01 YC43
Associated companies throughout the world
www.panmacmillan.com

ISBN 978-1-0350-3758-2

1 3 5 7 9 8 6 4 2

A CIP catalogue record for this book is available from the British Library.

Typeset in Adobe Caslon Pro by Palimpsest Book Production Ltd, Falkirk, Stirlingshire
Printed and bound by CPI Group (UK) Ltd, Croydon, CR0 4YY

Visit **www.panmacmillan.com** to read more about all our books
and to buy them. You will also find features, author interviews and
news of any author events, and you can sign up for e-newsletters
so that you're always first to hear about our new releases.

To Dad and Matt x

Contents

Prologue

My dress is a classic red lace Dolce & Gabbana. I bought it last week, along with a small black jacket, which the lady in the shop told me really 'finished off the look'. I check the mirror . . . I feel good, confident even. The lady was right, the jacket does pull it all together. My hair is up and I finish off with a red lipstick. I feel excited AND I feel nervous. I'm off to the Theatre Royal Drury Lane. It's a five-minute walk from my flat in Covent Garden. Tonight is the Olivier Awards and I have been nominated for best supporting role in a musical. I can't quite believe it's real, but it is and off I go. It's a beautiful balmy night in London.

Maybe I don't need the jacket? No, no, the lady said it looked great.

I arrive at the theatre and do the red carpet, something I usually hate, but tonight I feel good so I pose and smile and then walk into the foyer to meet my friends. We chat and giggle as we take our seats. The lights dim, the music plays and the ceremony begins. I'm starting to feel a bit edgy. I know my category is up fairly early on so I sit tight and tell myself the wait will be over soon. I feel really happy to be nominated, but to win? I wonder what that would feel like! I try not to get too distracted and before I know it the nominations are being read out. The winner of best supporting role in a musical goes to . . . Jill Halfpenny. I can't believe it. I genuinely didn't expect to hear my name. I'm shocked as I make my way up to the podium. I give my acceptance speech and off I walk into the winners' lounge! I'm thrilled, I'm delighted, and then things take a bit of a strange turn. I slowly begin to feel . . . well, the same? My new-found confidence of approximately sixty seconds ago is waning. I thought I would *feel* different, I thought people would *see* me differently, but I'm being interviewed and photographed by people who don't seem to be that bothered.

OK, I know what this is. I didn't win best lead role; I won best supporting role. Maybe when you win best lead role you will feel like you've arrived, maybe *that's* when people look at you differently.

The minutes roll by and I hear the next winner and the winner after that being announced. My time slot to be the most sought-after person in the room is running out. It's funny, though, they do seem to be really interested in talking to these new winners? The night continues in a blur of interviews, congratulatory hugs and calls to my family who are just so happy for me. In fact, they seem happier than I am? Somehow I can't shake off the feeling of not feeling changed. I expected to feel a sense of arrival, of belonging, of finally feeling as though I deserve a place at the table.

Exactly a week later I am outside the same theatre with my son Harvey. He is potty-training and he has pooed himself right on the steps of Drury Lane. He desperately wants to go to the park so I decide to change and clean him right there rather than go back home. Only a week ago I was picking up a beautiful bronze statue and now I'm picking up Harvey's poo. A few days later I see an article in a magazine. It's a 'who wore it better?' and it's me and Isla Fisher in the Dolce & Gabbana dress. She wins by a large margin. She isn't wearing the black jacket . . . Damn.

Dear reader, this isn't a book about the Oliviers or fancy dresses and ceremonies. This is about the journey I've been on with my grief and how I was in danger of letting it rob me of all my joy. How my trauma threatened to overshadow all the beautiful, precious moments in my life because it was left unprocessed and unattended to. I will share with you how I came to understand the leading role it played in my life. I desperately tried to outrun it, but it caught up with me. And thank God it did. This is the story of how I was finally able to accept myself by facing my grief and allowing myself to die a little.

PART 1
OPENING ACT

Chapter 1

Backstory

———

There was only one picture in the house of my dad. It was of him and a friend and it sat on my mam's bedside table. There were no other traces of him at home.

My dad, Colin Halfpenny, died on 9 August 1979. He was thirty-six years old. My mam, Maureen, was thirty-three. I had just turned four in July and I was about to start my first year at St Augustine's primary school. I remember nothing from the day of his death – or maybe I do? To be honest, I have snippets from my sisters and Mam, but the actual details of how things unfolded still feel in many ways a mystery to me. Maybe that's because no one wanted to sit me down and talk through the details. Maybe it's because in times of great stress and trauma we can become unreliable narrators and therefore details and timings appear opaque and confusing. Maybe it's because I've never felt comfortable enough to talk through it. This is what I think I know . . .

It was a Sunday. (I have since checked with Mam – it was Thursday evening!)

Dad was playing football for a local league.

He ate some cheese and crackers (that's a detail from my big sis Nicola). Then left the house having had a little tiff with my mam. She was frustrated he was leaving to play a friendly match. She thought it was unnecessary and wanted him home. He said he had to go, it was important. Mam sporadically refers to this bickering and follows it with, 'Never leave the house on an argument, Jill.' I think it's haunted her that her last words weren't loving.

In the middle of the match Dad went in for a tackle, collided with another player, collapsed, had a heart attack and died. My dad's brother was there, he witnessed the whole ordeal, an ambulance was called, and Dad was pronounced dead on the pitch. It really is no exaggeration to say that I don't know if any of these details are totally correct. That day is vague and the specifics muddy even to my eldest sister, who was ten at the time. There were three of us girls: myself, four; Paula, seven; and Nicola, ten.

For forty-four years I had stared at a stretch of grass in Leam Lane park thinking, believing, that was where Dad died. I was only told about a year ago while at a storage unit with my sister that the area of car park we could see about fifty metres away used to be a gated pitch area and that was where Dad died.

'Really,' I said. '*There?*'

'Yeah,' my sister said matter-of-factly. 'Apparently the gate to the pitch was locked and the paramedics couldn't get their vehicle into the grounds to reach Dad.'

I was almost embarrassed to tell her that I'd been staring at that playing field in Leam Lane park for all those years, wondering what he might have looked like lying there motionless on the grass. Leam Lane park was two minutes from my school. It sat behind the swimming baths, where I would go with my mates before grabbing a pasty from Greggs. Later in my life it became a place to hang out with a bottle of cider. There was an area of grass to the right of the play park where I would sometimes see football games being played. I have no idea how I came to believe that this was the place Dad died, but I did, and I must never have questioned it.

I was gobsmacked. Not about the detail itself but the fact that I'd never heard it before.

I recently spoke to Mam about the unfolding of that day and the weeks and months that followed – and she too was hazy. What she was able to tell me was that she received a knock at the door from a policeman. She was told Dad had been in a fatal accident and she had to go and identify his body at the mortuary. We were taken next door to our neighbour, Margaret. Mam was alone at the mortuary and my uncle Derek had to go to his parents' house to tell them their son, his brother, was dead. Mam said she remembers coming home but she didn't recall exact details of what she said to us or how it was done. I pushed her to try to remember. She said she vaguely remembers saying Dad had been in an accident and he wouldn't be coming back. He was gone. When I asked how we reacted, she said, 'You seemed happy with what you'd been told.' What she meant is that we seemed to understand. We seemed to have a grasp on the news.

It feels to me like that day was played out separately between each of my two sisters, my mam, my uncle and myself, and there has never been a time when we have all sat down to piece it together. To make a timeline of sorts, to try to make it make sense. I get it . . . why on earth would anyone want to replay the worst day of their life, right?! But I look back now and I wish I did know exactly what had happened, to have some clarity and structure. For so long it's been steeped in mystery. A black day never to be mentioned or spoken about.

It was decided that the children wouldn't go to the funeral. The general consensus was that it would be too difficult for us. Who made this decision and where we went during the ceremony is not something I remember. What I do remember is that Dad's body was kept in the cupboard next door to the living room. It's a walk-in space used for coats and shoes. The coffin stayed in there for a couple of days before the funeral. The door was slightly ajar and I have a vague recollection of looking at it and feeling scared.

I remember sitting on my nana's knee when people came back to the house. I can smell her cigarette-soaked clothes and I can feel a very strange air all around me. Whatever is happening doesn't feel good but I don't quite know what it is. Mam said she stayed upstairs in the bedroom. She could hear people talking downstairs and seemingly sounding OK. 'No one feels the way I feel,' she thought. 'No one must be in this much pain if they can sit downstairs and chat.' She recently admitted to me that this was how she felt for a very long time. Absolutely no one, including us, her children who had lost their father, could feel as bad as she did because everyone else seemed 'fine'.

Her grief became more private and internal. There was only one picture in the house of my dad. It was of him and a friend and it sat on my mam's bedside table. There were no other traces of him at home. No pictures of us as a family, on holiday. Nothing. It was as if he was erased.

Many anniversaries passed without any special emphasis. When one of us would say we were going to the graveyard to lay flowers we would often be met with 'no need, I've done it, they'll only go to waste or get blown away'.

Mam admitted to me that she felt if we weren't reminded of him then it would be easier to live without him. She believed it would somehow erase our pain.

Unfortunately, what happened was that by removing all traces of him and rarely mentioning him – by not celebrating his birthday or acknowledging our loss – she made a case for her own beliefs. She believed no one hurt as much as she did and so, without realizing it, our family never learnt how to grieve together, we never showed each other our pain. And her beliefs came true.

The truth is my mam was completely lost. She was heart-broken and she had no idea how she was going to cope. If she could get out of bed to feed us, clothe us and send us to school then that was a good day. She didn't have counselling or friends to connect deeply with. She had family who offered solid practical support. Her parents helped and her sister Joan moved in with us for a while. We needed to survive, so we did as so many families do and we 'just got on with it'. Our lives kept moving forward, kept changing, and there was very little reflection. We became a family of doers! We threw ourselves into being busy. It was fun; there was always something going on and Mam was our biggest cheerleader in everything we turned our hand to. She was always there supporting us and encouraging our passions. The 'doing' stopped the 'feeling', so it was only when

13

things slowed down and got quiet that I felt as though something was missing.

As I've said, I don't remember a lot, but I do have one very clear memory. I have no idea how many weeks or months it was after Dad's death.

I was outside playing in the street. I came into the house and I heard someone laughing. It sounded strange, maniacal. Like those sinister laughing policemen at the fair. I ran into the front room and peeked through the door. My mam was hugging my uncle. Laughing. I stayed there for what seemed like a few minutes before I realized this was actually wailing – big, guttural wails. My uncle's eyes landed on mine. They locked and I was gently shooed away with his hand. I didn't ask why or where I should go. I just knew I needed to. I wasn't welcome there; this wasn't meant for my eyes or ears.

It must have made a fairly profound impact, because I remember it so vividly. How I felt – unwelcome, intrusive. To this day if I get any sort of sense that I've outstayed my welcome somewhere I'm off like a shot. Maybe I took the shooing to heart and felt like I wasn't welcome in my mam's grief. Perhaps I wasn't?

The next bit of clarity I have is playing a game with my middle sister, Paula. I'm six now and she's nine. The game was 'run into the front room and say "Dad" and then run away'. This wasn't because we were hoping he would come back; it was because there was a new man in there. A familiar one too. My dad's brother Derek (my uncle), who had witnessed Dad's death on the pitch that evening. He had fallen in love with my mam and moved into the family home because they were about to get married. My sister and I were daring each other to go into the room and allow the word 'Dad' to be directed to a new man in our lives.

On 4 September 1981, my mam and Derek married. I was a bridesmaid. I remember my dress very clearly. I had worn it for my auntie's wedding earlier that year. It was pink with very small flowers on it. My auntie Joan had given me and my cousin Joanne small bags to carry rather than bouquets. They were cute little purses with drawstrings. When I was Mam's bridesmaid I begged her to let me carry a bouquet. I wanted to feel grown up and sophisticated. Mam and Derek married in our local church. When we went into the vestry to sign the papers after the ceremony we all huddled together and cried. I wasn't sure why at the time but I joined in anyway. On reflection, I imagine the tears were a true mix of the bittersweet feelings of that day. Mam and Derek had fallen for each other, they wanted to be married, but we all knew that this was born out of tragedy. Mam told me that she had received some negativity about her relationship with Derek from friends and family. I don't think she felt fully supported that day. Derek made a promise to look after us all and bring us up as his own. We all called him Dad and still do to this day, but so as not to confuse you, the reader, I will refer to Derek as my stepdad.

I'm sure it will come as no surprise to hear that I was an anxious kid. I really didn't like school and I would feel sick almost every morning. My mam would beg me to eat breakfast but all I ever managed was a Rich Tea biscuit. My stomach would be in knots. I hated leaving her and if she was a few minutes late to pick me up I'd be freaking out. Dad died in August and I started school in September. It seems pretty likely I had abandonment issues and separation anxiety – I feared Mam would be gone as suddenly as Dad. On top of not having a space to express my grief, having to leave Mam every day and not knowing if she would return at pick-up was a daily struggle. I don't remember much detail, I only remember the feeling. The nervousness in my belly, which felt like butterflies, the lack of appetite and the general feeling of 'not knowing'.

I would break up my day into segments in my head. The first would be to see if I could get to milk break. I could have a biscuit then and I would be hungry by that time. The next was lunch. Lunch meant it was nearer to home time. I could enjoy the sandwiches Mam had made for me. The white bread with the hard cheese and the fruit and nut Club biscuit. After lunch there was usually a PE lesson and I liked PE, and then there was only an hour or so left before home time. Breaking it up felt more manageable, more bearable. The quicker I could get home and know everything was OK, the better. This was the way it played out every day.

My mam was as patient as she could be but after a very long time she became frustrated. She thought I just didn't like school or was having trouble with friends. The truth is my grief was still stuck and I was finding life and school hard. I felt different, separate, weird. I hadn't found my people yet and I was a constant worrier. I'd panic if my homework wasn't done – even now I can't stand the thought of doing anything wrong or being in trouble. There were a couple of girls who were mean to me and I didn't have the confidence to not care. I cared so deeply. I was highly sensitive, my skin felt raw.

I'm nine now, it's Sunday night and I'm sitting at the kitchen bench, watching Mam prepare the packed lunches. I can feel the familiar knot in my stomach and the overwhelm of sickness. 'I don't want to go to school.' Mam takes a deep breath as I watch her trying to garner some patience for the endless repetition of Sunday night anxiety. She looks at me and asks calmly, 'Why?'

'I don't know, I just don't.'

She takes the knife and slams it down hard on the kitchen bench and then turns and runs upstairs, to the bathroom. I've never seen her like this before and I'm scared. I follow upstairs to find her slumped against the bath, crying. She's exhausted, she's trying her best, she wants me to be OK. But she's at a loss. I'm watching her cry and for the first time I'm seeing this woman, who I rely on for everything, who listens to me and tucks me in at night and tries her absolute best to do what's right, and she is all out of answers and I feel sick. I've done this to her. I've brought her to her knees and I've broken her. I've broken my mam. I tell her I'm sorry and we cry together on the bathroom floor. My mam is exhausted with her grief and she is trying to hold it all together for the sake of her family. Neither of us is right or wrong, we're just in a moment. A moment that needed to happen. That was the first time I remember seeing my mam as a vulnerable human being and not just my super mam. It helped, it made me feel less alone and I understood. Maybe I had been pushing for a reaction like that to check if she was human. To see if what was inside me was inside her too?

As I grew older my pain found other ways to escape. Later, as a teenager, it discovered alcohol, which I will talk about later, but at ten years old it found dancing. I joined a small local class that a neighbour had recommended, and it was my haven. My grief was stuck inside me. And my ten-year-old body had gravitated towards what it needed without even knowing it. From the outside, it looked as if I just loved performing and showing off. On the inside, I needed to move and to shift all the pain. I would dance incessantly in my bedroom. The room was directly above the living room and at least twice a day I would hear screams from my mam: 'Jill! The chandelier!' (We lived in a council house with low ceilings. We had a light with three bulbs in it but for some reason Mam called it a chandelier!) I had bought myself a cassette of Richard Clayderman. It was full of piano ballads. I would throw myself around the bedroom, crying, sobbing, being very dramatic and quite impressive, and then I'd collapse on my bean bag, exhausted, feeling like a prima ballerina at the end of *Swan Lake*.

I can see clearly now that I was grieving. I was giving myself a way to let my feelings out. A way that felt acceptable. A way that was solitary and a way (apart from the chandelier) that didn't disturb anyone.

I know now that grief always finds a way to escape, often in disguise. My family's private grief made me feel isolated, so I was left to make sense of it and I came up with some pretty shameful thoughts about myself, one of which was: *If I am OK in my life, I can't have really loved my dad. I am not sad enough, so that makes me a bad person.*

Dear reader, here are some things I've learnt:

Mam

The day before writing this, I again asked Mam something I've been asking her throughout my life. Something that always upset and confused me: what was Dad *like*? I wanted to get a picture of him, maybe a few anecdotes about our relationship and how he felt about me. Anything I could get to hold on to. She would often give the same reply: 'Well, he wasn't what you'd call a dad's dad. He wouldn't read bedtime stories or anything like that. He was busy and had lots of hobbies.'

To say this would blindside me is an understatement. I would ask the same question every few years hoping for a different answer, but the same one would come out. I just couldn't get my head around it. Why would she say that?

When we spoke about it very recently, she said it was the truth. I asked: would it be the truth to say 'he loved me'? Would it be true to say 'he was overjoyed when I was born and he adored me'?

'Absolutely,' she replied.

So why tell me something negative, then? Why tell me something that makes me feel further away from him?

She looked at me as she reflected. I could see her trying to work out why. She looked sad, regretful. 'I suppose,' she said, 'I thought if I told you that, it would make you miss him less.'

I don't want to demonize my mam in any way. She was left with three children and no career to speak of. She did her best with what she was given and she was an excellent mam in so many ways. But I needed to tell you this to help in understanding the decisions we make when we are deep in grief. To demonstrate how important it is to deal with not only ourselves, but also the people who have also lost loved ones, with extreme care. Comments and conversations can linger for lifetimes. When you're heartbroken and someone delivers you a sucker punch, it takes a lot to get the courage back up to ask for help again. We suffer in silence. How many of you reading this book have lived with a belief and not been brave enough to question it for fear of getting your heart broken all over again?

Speaking to Mam about it now, she can absolutely see how this was unhealthy and made it incredibly difficult for us to deal with the loss, but she said that at the time she felt if she could take away all the pain and reminders for us then we would have a better chance at moving on and being happy. This makes my heart break for her. The things we do to protect others and to protect ourselves. She was a woman in a situation so unfamiliar and frightening that she went into survival mode. For herself and her family. She wanted to believe the silence would mean it would go away. Like a little girl just praying it would all disappear. She was doing what she thought was right at the time. Unfortunately, this is not how grief works.

I feel certain that we were not OK. The words that our beloved dad was dead and never coming back must have been incredibly shocking. When we are traumatized, as my mam was, we find it very hard to be able to hold other people's trauma too. It's just too much. My mam was in shock. She said she kept thinking, *What am I going to do? How will I cope?*

There was no support or professional advice – no 'let's talk about our feelings' or memory jars. It seems inconceivable now. It's so hard for me (and my mam) to understand that this was the approach that was deemed best. It was a different time and everyone was doing what they needed to survive.

I understand the intention and the thought process. *Let's not upset the kids by having pictures of their dad around the house. It will make them feel worse. Let's not remind them of what they have lost.* But I didn't need a picture to remind me of what I had lost; I was aware of that every single day and still am. It lives in me. Pictures are powerful; they evoke memories and encourage conversation. Keeping Dad alive with pictures and stories would have helped us all to process the man we loved and lost. It would have helped us to keep the sadness and pain present and breathing rather than shutting it away. We would have learnt that grief can live alongside happiness if it's dealt with carefully. He was removed because it was mistakenly believed to be easier. This way of dealing with grief leads to confusion and complications. It encouraged me to swallow, to bury, to disassociate. Which led me to so much more nefarious behaviour in the future. I didn't know where to put my pain, there wasn't a place for it, so it hung in the air and it lived in my body – my little four-year-old body – and it stayed there until it turned itself into things that could be understood more easily. Anxiety, nightmares and a voracious need to please.

In keeping her grief to herself, Mam tried to minimize Dad to all of us and kept a giant-sized version of him to herself. Unfortunately, this coping strategy meant that we lost out on grieving as a family. We lost out on the ability to share and connect with each other. We didn't have the opportunity to grow closer in our pain. We allowed it to push us apart. We stayed close physically and practically but not emotionally. It was very confusing growing up in a household where grief was front and centre but never directly talked about. It felt unsettling. My external world, which was full of love and care, didn't match up with my anxious, untethered internal world. Trying to make sense of this as a child was almost impossible, so I turned it inward and blamed myself, and that's where the shame began. I couldn't make sense of it so I presumed it must be me.

We all learnt how to grieve silently. We all learnt how to take our pain and place it into another area of our lives where it could lurk and metastasize. We didn't know how to grieve in the open. We weren't shown how to do that. We thought we weren't allowed.

Masking grief

Because our family grief wasn't openly talked about, I developed into a highly sensitive child; I could *feel* and *sense* if something was wrong. If I was told 'it's nothing, everything's fine', it confused me. My feeling didn't match the words I was being told so I began to distrust (myself mainly), which then led to anxiety. I became a detective in my life, always wondering whether what people were feeling and what they were saying matched up. It was *exhausting*.

We often hide our pain from our children. We think we're protecting them. We lie and say things like, 'Oh, I've had a bad day at work' or 'I've fallen out with Nana'. I always think honesty is best. If you're hurting, let your children know you're in pain but assure them you will be OK. That way they can learn that pain is not something to be scared of and, more importantly, you can survive it. Loss of some kind is inevitable. If we can be open about how we feel then we can give our children the chance to watch the process as we journey through it. Even now, as an adult, I can be too quick to try to pull myself out of pain. Sometimes my need to move on out of the discomfort means I drag the residue along behind me rather than processing it properly in the first place.

Abandoned

It seems so obvious when I write this that I had abandonment issues.

The culture felt very different at the time. Now, a child might be assigned a counsellor at school. They would be offered support. There are charities and support groups that work solely with bereaved families, but back then, certainly where we were, there wasn't any of that offered to us.

What was missing from my development was an understanding adult or therapist who could guide me through these feelings. Essentially, we were all left to grieve and find our path through this alone.

Up until my late teens I thought that maybe I'd 'got away with it', but I soon learnt that you can't outrun grief. It will wait patiently for you until you're ready to pay attention to it. And until then it will reveal itself as anger, depression, addiction or busyness and it will show up all the time in your interpersonal relationships.

I feel it's important for me to stress that, despite all of this, I did have many, many happy times in my childhood. Grief can live alongside fun and laughter.

Caravan holidays – snuggled up playing cards together, betting with pennies as it rained outside and Mam made us cheese on toast. I loved playing in the street – we'd have huge games of hide and seek that would go on for whole weekends! My mam was chief organizer for our cul-de-sac and she would hire coaches so we could go on a day trip to the coast. We'd sing songs on the back seat at the top of our voices: 'Geoooooordie had a pigeon a pigeon a pigeon.' The friends I made at dance school were so funny and up for a laugh. We would dress up in daft outfits, dare each other to go to the shop and order something in a different accent. Always happy to make fools of ourselves. We were in no hurry to 'grow up'. Jokes, laughter and boisterousness certainly co-existed with sadness. I knew I had to survive the pain, and kids are brilliant at intuitively knowing what they need to do to survive. I hopped in and out of my grief like puddles and only stayed in each place until I'd had enough. My struggles came when I stopped listening to my intuition, when my head took over and I believed I didn't need to take care of the sadness.

Chapter 2

Getting on with it

———

Each production I performed in cemented the feeling that acting was exactly what I wanted to do . . . It felt like it was mine and I was in control.

I was a hungry little girl. Hungry for everything. I wanted more biscuits, more fun, more friends, more love and more acceptance. God, I was hungry for acceptance. The more I got, the more I wanted. I was an empty bucket, always trying to fill myself up but never feeling satisfied.

I loved a busy day. I thrived on stress and overstimulation. A perfect day would be dance lessons in the morning, rehearsals for a production throughout the afternoon and then a sleepover at a friend's house in the evening. I loved every minute to be taken up with doing. I didn't want to stop until it was time to sleep and when I did go to bed I wanted to feel exhausted so that I would fall asleep immediately.

I hated, *loathed*, Sundays. Sundays were quiet, Sundays were empty. On Sundays you could hear your own head and that was scary. Sundays included church, which was boring. I joined the choir so I could sit upstairs and at least pass the time singing. Then it was a quick visit to Nana's; it was pretty dull there but she made a great scone, so at least I could look forward to that. Then back home to cook the Sunday dinner. Sunday dinners made me feel sick – the mashed potato, the soggy veg from the pressure cooker and the smell of turnip wafting through the house as Barbra Streisand blasted from the hi-fi. (At least there was Barbra!) As I sat down late afternoon to eat the dinner I would be aware that time was ticking and soon it would be bath and bed and then the dreaded school.

Sundays were the precursor to the separation anxiety that began on Monday morning. My dread, my need to please, to be accepted, to feel normal. It's difficult, because I think my busyness sometimes looked like happiness. Part of me *was* thriving. I LOVED all the doing. But there was a little part of me that was also dying.

My dancing classes kept me very busy but were also a saving grace for my grief. It helped to release all the stuck energy inside my body, and the friends I made there were the ones I have to this day. They were my tribe, no doubt about it. It was where I felt I most belonged. Without it and without them, my life would have been a lot scarier and emptier. There was always so much going on at dance school. I was there at least three times a week and we would prepare for competitions, exams and performances. A lot of looking forward, planning, propelling. It suited me down to the ground. No reflection or hours of boredom on my own to think. Just doing, doing, doing.

The dance school was situated within the church grounds, just off a dual carriageway. To the right was the beautiful old church and its graveyard and to the left was a new graveyard, where my dad was buried. I could see his headstone from the dance class car park. I find it interesting that I spent so many hours of my childhood so very close to him. I became inseparable with a girl I met at dancing called Helen; she lived directly opposite the churchyard. I spent so much time at her house and

I would often look out of her bedroom window and wonder if he could see or hear me.

The school consisted of four separate rooms. The biggest one housed a small stage where we would do end-of-term perform-ances. It was cold a lot of the time and had no luxury to speak of. I loved it. My teacher was called Mrs Reavley (Sandra), and her husband Ron would take our cash at the door. Sandra was strict and didn't overly enthuse, but nevertheless you knew when you had pleased her. She would give you a little smile and nod and off you'd go. They were a two-man band but it always felt bigger than that. Maybe it was the enthusiasm of all us kids, but for such a small school we did really well in competitions and exams. I did a lot of ballet, stage and modern. I never really liked the ballet; it was so difficult and I didn't feel graceful enough, but looking back now I think it served me well. It gave me discipline and strength and the ability to be uncomfortable. Ballet always felt painful to me, but I learnt that if you stay with the pain and work on the technique it becomes easier and your body surpasses your expectations. Without knowing, I was learning a lesson in grief that would become imperative for me.

My mam seemed to love my dancing too. She had lots of friends there and they enjoyed each other's company. Mam is a talented seamstress so it wasn't long before she was making all my costumes for dance comps, as well as for anyone else who asked! She would put a huge amount of effort into them and I always felt so proud, she was my clever mam!

Dance school felt happy and exciting and like a definite

escape from the mundanity of home. I continued keeping busy throughout my childhood. I was involved in lots of productions within my region and, as much as I loved dancing, I began to realize I needed something more. I was cast in a local panto, we got fifty pence a performance and then a raise to a quid the next year! I loved being involved but I would watch the principals rehearse, scripts in hand, and I would feel jealous. I wanted to be with them. I wanted to have lines and a character name.

I was ten by now and I knew for sure I didn't want to be in the background any more. There was an advertisement in the back of our local paper, the *Chronicle*, asking kids to audition for a new production of *Sweeney Todd* at the Newcastle Playhouse. Helen and I decided to go for it. We had a similar gung-ho attitude and we were always up for new experiences. Once, at dancing school, we'd decided we couldn't be bothered to do our ballet lesson, so we hid in the large storage cupboard, jumped up and down on the trampette and scoffed the tuck shop sweets!

So when we saw that ad, off we went on the Metro to an open casting for *Sweeney Todd*. We were asked to sing 'Happy Birthday' solo and then read a few bits of script. We both got the job and we were thrilled!

It was directed by Ken Hill. An intimidating man but I loved him. I wanted to impress him. I got to play a few different parts in the show. I was a street urchin as Tobias sold Pirelli's miracle elixir. I was the kid of a family in the pie shop when Mrs Lovett's business began to boom. There was a bakery in

Newcastle called Carricks, which would supply the pies each night. They were really big and round and had loads of pastry on the crust. I loved that scene, I so enjoyed eating the pies and singing loudly with a mouth full. Singing and eating, two of my favourite things!

In another scene I had to play a girl who was taken along to the barber's by her father. By this point Sweeney Todd was killing people for his pies and my father was prime meat. The problem was, Sweeney wasn't able to go through with it because I was watching him, smiling sweetly and innocently every time we caught each other's eye. The scene was macabre but funny, the audience sniggering every time Sweeney, who was mid-shave, couldn't quite finish the deed and slash my father's neck. I loved playing it because it was effectively improvised. Ken had told us what was needed but hadn't been too specific with timings etc. I could play with the actor and we could have our own rhythm – that was thrilling to me. After a dress rehearsal one evening, I was waiting in the foyer to go home and my chaperone took me to one side.

'I was sitting next to Ken when you were performing the shaving scene,' she said.

Oh no, I thought, fearing I was about to get a director's note from him about what I was doing wrong. He was notorious for the specificity of his notes.

She continued: 'He leaned over to me and said, "That girl is going to be famous one day."'

I felt a surge of adrenaline fill my body. *Ken Hill believes in me!!!*

It felt like such an audacious thing to say, and up until that point no adult had ever shown that kind of belief in me.

I worked with Ken again on his next show, *The Silver Chair*. He had also cast a young Julia Sawalha. She was mesmerizing, I just loved her. I would go home each night after rehearsals and try to emulate everything I'd seen her do. One of my characters was a mouse. I wore red velvet pedal pushers, a white frilly blouse and a papier mâché mouse head. I loved wearing that mask; it made me feel braver and more daring on stage.

Each production I performed in cemented the feeling that acting was exactly what I wanted to do. It was becoming my dream. I began to realize that acting did something for me that nothing else had come close to. Dancing had helped me move my body and release myself from the constriction of grief, but acting – acting felt way more autonomous. It felt like it was mine and I was in control. Without knowing, I was gravitating to a space where I could control the narrative of my grief more. Once the characters were mine, I could shape and mould them to express themselves in a way that made sense to me. It felt right.

By the age of thirteen I had joined a drama club and I had an agent, named Dave Holly. One day he called to say I had an audition for *Byker Grove*. I was so excited. Over the years I would lament to my mam over and over again, 'I wish there was a Geordie *Grange Hill*!' It's no exaggeration to say that there was little to no children's drama being filmed up in the North-East at that time, so all the shows I would watch like *Grange Hill* and *Jossy's Giants* felt far away.

I had to go to the Pink Palace, which was the nickname for

the pink BBC building in Fenham, Newcastle. For my first audition I had been given scenes to read for Spuggie. Spuggie was described as an innocent and slightly broken little girl. In the scene I'd been asked to read she was upset and being consoled by Mary O'Malley. I walked into a bright room on the top floor of the building. Matthew Robinson and Andy Snelgrove introduced themselves to me and I sat down and began to read Spuggie's scenes while Matthew filmed. I had no idea how the audition was going but at some point they stopped me, looked at each other, and then said to me, 'You're not a Spuggie, you're much more of a Nicola. Can you go outside and look over those scenes, please, and then come back in.' Nicola was older, more streetwise, and the best friend of Donna.

I was devastated. I was sure they were just asking me to read Nicola because they felt sorry for me and didn't want me to feel I'd wasted my time (clearly I didn't know the business then!). I had experienced quite a few knock-backs with auditions by this point. I never felt as though I was 'what they were looking for'. Not cute enough, not small enough, not blonde enough – basically I felt not good enough. I would get close and then get rejected. I sat outside the room and studied the scenes as another kid went in to do their audition. After about five minutes I was ushered back into the room. I was nervous; I had memorized Spuggie's lines but I would be sight-reading for Nicola. Nevertheless, I didn't show it. I had absorbed as much as possible and off I went. There was a line in one of the scenes that read, 'I like the more swinish types, Tom Cruise-ish, Jason Donovan-ish.'

I had never heard the word 'swinish' before. We did it a couple of times and I kept pronouncing it 'sweeeenish'.

'Do you know what that word means, Jill?' asked Matthew.

'No,' I said, embarrassed.

He explained and also gave me the correct pronunciation and off we went again. *Oh god*, I thought. *Not only am I not Spuggie enough, they're gonna think I'm stupid now and I can't read properly.*

They thanked me for my time and off I went, sure I had done badly. A week or so later, I get a call from my agent, Dave.

'Well done, you've got a recall. You'll be getting a letter explaining what will be required of you.'

The letter arrived saying the audition would take place back at the Pink Palace from ten to four on a Saturday. We would be auditioning together as a group and it would be a fun day as opposed to any pressure. We had to bring along a fun gift and we were to prepare a little performance lasting no more than five minutes. Anything we wanted. I decided to sing 'High Hopes'. The song was on a Frank Sinatra album my stepdad would often play. I liked it, so off I went to my bedroom and made up a little dance routine to it.

The day was fun. We played games and got to know each other but there was no sense of how you were doing so I left feeling none the wiser. I think, looking back, there were two of us for every part available and Matthew obviously wanted to see how we interacted with each other and who gelled with who, etc. I don't remember much about it apart from Sally McQuillan. She was a force – confident and funny. We would eventually be cast as best friends Nicola and Donna and I enjoyed every second of working with her.

We were told to expect a phone call the next day. I waited and waited. It was late afternoon by now and I was beginning to lose hope.

The phone rings. I answer.

'Hello, Jill, it's Matthew.'

'Hi, Matthew.'

'Did you enjoy yourself yesterday?'

Oh no, I think. *That's what people say before they give you bad news.*

'I did, thank you,' I reply.

'Well, I've done all my no's and now I'm on to my yes's.'

My heart stops and the world slows down. Is this really happening?

'We would love you to play the role of Nicola Dobson in *Byker Grove*. How d'you feel about that?'

'Fantastic,' I say.

He chats for a few minutes more but I don't really hear what he is saying. All I can think is that I'm going to be in a television programme, a Geordie *Grange Hill*, a drama where I will get to play my own character!

I put down the phone and I scream to my mam and stepdad, 'I got it, I got it, I got the part!'

And then something strange happens. I run towards the sofa and as I bounce up and down on it, my arms cheering in the air, I feel a very heavy familiar feeling in the pit of my stomach. I feel unbelievably sad and I start to disassociate.

I watch myself bouncing on the sofa and I tell myself that's what happy people do so I have to continue. It's so confusing. I KNOW I'm thrilled to have got the role, I KNOW I'm ecstatic at the thought of filming and being an actress, but I just don't FEEL it. It's as though my brain has put on the brakes, it can't handle the rush of emotion and it's taken me to a place that is more familiar. A place it knows. It's as if it doesn't want to get too excited or too happy because that's where disappointment lies. If I love something too much, then might it be taken away from me? All I know is that I've been given some of the most exciting news that I could possibly think of and my brain/body has grabbed me by the scruff of the neck and pulled me back to a place where joy isn't welcome. A place where it can be back in control. Where it's safer and there is less chance of being let down. I feel frightened and confused . . . a familiar state for me.

However, as the weeks roll on, and much to my relief, I begin to be able to absorb the news without feeling over-whelmed and it starts to feel very real. I allow myself to get excited, really, really excited, and then I embark on a chapter of my story that will turn out to be one of the most exhilarating of my life.

I'm thirteen, it's my first day on set. I'm being picked up by my runner in a red Mondeo. It's Si King (before he was a Hairy Biker!). He's funny and warm. We're filming outside a news-agent. I'm excited and nervous. It all goes well and without a hitch. Matthew says I'm a natural and I feel proud. Considering it's my first experience I feel strangely comfortable on the set.

The boom, the camera, the lights, none of them bother me. I feel at home. I love the 6 a.m. pick-ups, the ten-hour days, the hair, the make-up, the costume, the green room – it all feels so different and so intoxicating. We film in a huge old building called The Mitre. The whole look and vibe of the place is different to anything I've experienced. It's the opposite of our home. It's huge, it's intriguing, and it's full to the brim of creative people. I'm exposed to a creative smorgasbord! Everyone from the runners to the make-up artists, the production designers to the camera crew, all feel so exotic to me and I LOVE it. I feel truly alive!

When the show airs, however, it's complex. I'm proud, so, so proud of the work I have done, but I struggle with the attention and the comments at school.

'Seen you on the telly last night . . . It was shit.'

It was 1988, in an urban school in Gateshead. If people were impressed, they never told me, or maybe it's that I only remember the negative comments. The constant attention, the whispering, the shouting at me on the school bus all took a toll and yet, despite all of that, it was never enough to make me feel like giving up. What it did do, unfortunately, was encourage me to make myself small whenever it felt necessary.

I did four seasons of *Byker*, I adored each one, and by the time I filmed my last episode at seventeen, I was on course to finish my A levels and then head to drama school. Throughout my time on *Byker*, I often wondered what Dad would have made of it. I've a hunch it would have been right up his street.

The experience of *Byker* only confirmed my desire to become an actress. It was a defining time in my life. I loved every second. We would film for about five months of the year but if we could have filmed all year round I would have said yes in a heartbeat. It was all-consuming (my favourite thing)! But all good things come to an end and the ending of *Byker* certainly hit me hard. My character was grown up now, and as it was set in a youth club it was time to make way for the younger cast. It felt like I was leaving a family behind. I was ready to spread my wings and yet the comfort of the *Byker* bubble was difficult to tear myself away from. I knew it was a significant ending and I was aware it was making way for new beginnings, but nevertheless I felt a huge loss inside. *Byker* helped me to grow, socially and professionally; it gave me purpose and it allowed me to truly believe that I could make a living out of doing something I love. To leave all that felt like a fissure. Even if I went back to visit I knew it would never be the same. I didn't want to be a visitor, I wanted to be IN it, and now I knew I would only be a part of its history. I cried of course on my last day and I knew even then that this would always be a very special time in my life.

I had been auditioning for drama schools for the last six months or so and I was over the moon to have been offered a place before I left the show. Thankfully, that gave me a new focus and softened the blow ever so slightly.

This feeling of loss was a familiar one, and throughout my childhood I battled with endings. The first time I became aware of this, I was eleven and I was involved in a production of *Annie* at the Tyne theatre and opera house. At the initial audition I had lost out on the role and I was devastated. I was performing in a pantomime at the time at the same theatre. Unbeknown to me, the girl I lost out to had dropped out and they were looking for someone to play one of the orphans, Kate.

One evening while I was performing the panto, Jack Dickson, our artistic director, was watching out front. Apparently he wanted to watch me perform before he made a decision. That night, after the show, I was told that he was offering me the role and rehearsals would begin immediately. I was elated. My mam printed off my script at the library – the toner was really dark and I couldn't see all of the lines properly but it didn't matter, it was mine! I put a staple at the top of my pages and off I went to rehearsals. I remember lying on the stage, in the opening scene at the orphanage, the floor felt cold on my cheek as I clutched my script listening to the opening number 'Maybe'. As I lay there I thought to myself, *There is nowhere else I would rather be right now.* I felt so happy to be part of the show and lapped up every moment of rehearsals.

Once we opened, the whole run was pure joy for me and by the night of the final performance, I was inconsolable, bereft. We all took to the stage for the final curtain call and I was crying so much that the other kids' parents noticed and commented on it. I seem to remember they made light of it and presumed it was simply because I had loved doing the show. I had, but I could sense even then my reaction seemed disproportionate to the event. The idea of it not being in my life was really hard. I loved all of it. The journey to the stage door, the pre-show chat and laughs, the performance and reaction of the audience, the interval snacks and just the general camaraderie. It was going to leave a gaping hole. It was going to be quiet again and everything was going to go back to normal, and it scared me.

This happened all through my school years. I noticed it whenever I was preparing for an exam or a performance, putting all my efforts and focus into it – when it was done I was always scared at how empty I felt, the feeling of things running out, stopping.

My mam was attentive, loving and kind but deep grief needs space and we were all too busy to let that happen. I was still like an empty bucket; I was trying to fill myself up with external pleasures, achievements and busyness. I had no idea that the way to fill this bucket would be to slow down, do less and take notice of what was happening inside me. This wasn't information or language I had been introduced to yet so I kept filling it up quickly and I felt exhausted. I couldn't understand why the satisfaction was so brief. No sooner had I received the great score in my dance exam or finished a particularly difficult scene on set than the feeling of 'do more, do better' would creep in. Holding on to satisfaction was the missing piece. I had no problem feeling it, but it was fleeting and I was left with the dread of needing to get it somewhere else. I thought I thrived on being busy, but what I really needed was balance, and I hadn't found it yet.

I had struggled with a negative internal dialogue – voices in my head – ever since I can remember. It never went away; it only became more or less exaggerated at different times of my life. I must have been about nine when I went through a phase of constantly apologizing. Whatever happened, even if I was to brush past someone's shoulder at school so gently they didn't notice, I would have to say sorry. Often I said it very quietly so as not to be heard, because I knew it was unnecessary and it would probably bring me unwanted attention if people heard me – but I had to know I had said it otherwise I would be an even worse person.

This was shame in all its glory. This was my unprocessed grief trying to find an outlet. The sad feelings inside of me that hadn't been given a space to express themselves were now attacking me. If you feel bad for long enough, one of the ways you may try to make sense of it is to turn it on yourself, and that's what I did.

My sisters and I all displayed obsessive behaviours and they all manifested at some point after Dad's death. My eldest sister, Nicola, would have to touch the garden gate in a certain ordered pattern every time she left the house; if she didn't, she thought something bad would happen. My middle sister, Paula, developed tics. One of them was a compulsive need to stretch her neck – she said she'd felt as though something was stuck in her throat and she was trying to release it as she stretched. It may seem strange, but we used to tease each other about our 'stuff'. We would laugh at each other, not really understanding what was happening. Of course we see it all now, but back then we were just living it.

My negative inner voices actually became my driver. The louder they were the more I wanted to prove them wrong. They would tell me I wasn't good enough. They taunted me with feelings of unworthiness. They liked to tell me I didn't belong in this world, that I was wrong and I didn't fit. They were very punitive and I'd often feel ashamed of who I was – I didn't have to *do* anything wrong; I simply *was* wrong. But it wasn't until I left for drama school and to live on my own that they began to really ramp up.

Chapter 3

Drama school and London

———

I was always searching for something.
I mistook this for ambition. I would think:
I just need more work, that's
all. Work will fix me.

I was eighteen when I left home for London. The school was called Webber Douglas and the building was in a swanky part of west London, surrounded by mews and beautiful flower-lined town houses. The place itself was pretty basic and consisted of a few different buildings all within five minutes' walk of each other. I was so excited to be going there, and to be living in London. It really was a dream of mine.

I had been drinking for a couple of years by this point and from seventeen onwards I was in bars and clubs with all my friends. When I went out I liked to get really drunk. I saw it as an adventure. The more drunk I got the greater the adventure. Always more. I couldn't settle for OK. Every night out had to be the *best* laugh, the *most* fun.

We didn't have a lot of money at drama school so a night out at the local pub or a house party were always my favourites. I loved house parties. You always had the best conversations there. You could dance, chat, be stupid and no one cared. It was also pretty handy if you couldn't afford a cab home. Just sleep on the floor and get the Tube back in the morning.

Alongside the party girl Jill was a truly motivated young woman. I had a vision for my future. I would be a successful actress and I wouldn't settle for anything less. If anything, my drive was only growing. I was still incredibly hungry, and ambition was very attractive to the hungry ghosts that lived inside me. They propelled me forward and let me believe there was always more to do: 'I mustn't rest on my laurels or slow down!'

I was doing everything that was asked of me and also having fun when I could. Drama school was as intense as it comes. The days were long and sometimes involved weekends. I loved it but also struggled. My teachers were harsh and not always encouraging.

The voices in my head had a party when I felt as though some teachers didn't rate me. It made their case stronger and the voices taunted me, telling me I didn't deserve to be there and that everyone was laughing at me.

It's hard to describe the attitude of some of the teachers there but there was just a low-level sense of disinterest in me. There were some who I never felt believed in me, who seemed enamoured and distracted by the tall, beautiful people. In my third year, one of my acting teachers announced that we would be doing the play *The Man of Mode*, a Restoration comedy. We read the play and familiarized ourselves with all the characters. We then had to write down on a card the character that we thought we would most likely be cast as and the one we thought we would be most unlikely to be cast as. The idea was that we would all be given a part that was unpredictable and stretched us in some way. These productions were internal. They are merely exercises to learn and grow as a performer. This acting teacher and I never got on. I thought she was grandiose and arrogant and she never seemed happy or impressed by anything I brought to the table. *This is interesting*, I thought. *Finally I'll get the chance to play something out of my age range or casting type and show her what I'm capable of.*

The character I'd written I would most likely be cast as was called Busy, a maid. The character I would least likely be cast as was Lady Townley. A few weeks later, the cast list had been decided. Not everyone had been given their most unlikely casting but they nearly all had been given something different or challenging. All except me and one other girl. I was given – yep, you guessed it – Busy. I think this may have been the first time that I was truly livid at drama school. I was hurt, I was embarrassed, but most of all I was angry. Suddenly I saw the bigger picture and even though I felt humiliated to be ignored in that way, it was more that I was mad at not being given the chance to grow as the others were. We all paid the same fees, we all had ability and talent to get in there in the first place, it seemed so wrong to me to not be given the chance to stretch and grow and be challenged. As I said, this was an internal production, only shown to the other teachers and pupils within the school. I felt as though this teacher had no reason to do this other than a complete lack of interest in my growth as a performer.

Some teachers were obsessed with my accent. Telling me I would never work if I didn't get rid of it. They chose to ignore the fact that I'd been working since I was ten and, although they never said this outright, I presumed they thought the work that I had done was easy to dismiss as it was 'kids' stuff'. I argued that surely the whole point of acting is to be able to be different people, so rather than get rid of it, I just wanted to be able to work in as many different accents as possible. I felt misunderstood: I went to drama school because I was desperate to learn more. I had been lucky with the experience I'd had as a child but I wanted to go to a classical drama school and push myself in ways I hadn't had the chance to before. I resented the fact that they seemed to concentrate their energy on those who they thought would achieve. But I was used to swallowing feelings, so I did a pretty neat job of absorbing all their crap too. When you're an empty bucket there's always room for more.

It's important for me to add, though, that there were a few teachers who I learnt a great deal from and who really did believe in me. Kim Grant was a director who freelanced at the school and directed me in *Dancing at Lughnasa* by Brian Friel. He was so encouraging; he liked my work and I grew in confidence because of him. He reminded me that there was a place for me out there; he made me feel hopeful. Edward Clark, who taught movement, helped me to understand that the choices you make as regards physicality in a character are just as powerful as the words. He taught with humour and compassion (and introduced me to yoga). His classes always felt very inclusive and he made me feel seen. And Raphael Jago, the head of the school, who was on the panel at my first audition there, wished me every success when I sat opposite him before my final year was out, to tell him I was leaving early. I'd been given a fantastic opportunity to play the lead in a Hull Truck Theatre production and it was an opportunity that couldn't be missed.

I had a boyfriend at drama school. We got together in the second year. His name was Marc and he was supportive, a fantastic actor and really funny. We laughed a lot at the madness of it all and he helped me keep perspective when I was struggling. We made each other's time there so much more fun because, although we loved what we were doing, we kept a lighter grip on things for our own sanity. Marc was outwardly one of the most confident people I have ever met and I was definitely drawn to him because of that. It was my first experience of being in love and, although the grief of Dad was still very much there, it was able to take a back seat. The intensity of study and falling in love meant it was easily ignored. The three years went by in a flash and before I knew it I was out in the world being a fully grown-up actress.

The play I had been offered was called *Like a Virgin*. It was a show about teenage friendship, illness and a devotion to Madonna! It was perfect casting for me and it set me up to be seen by lots of industry people when we took it to the Edinburgh Festival. We were in the Assembly Rooms and Gerard Butler was performing in there too with *Trainspotting*. We used to chat after our shows in the bar. Years later I was with my mam and we bumped into him on a Tube platform. We chatted and then off he went. I turned to my mam and she looked quite overcome. I think that's one of the first times I've seen anyone starstruck! It really made me laugh.

Work in those early years was tough. All the young graduates are fighting for the same roles. I was lucky enough to be cast in all of the TV shows I'd grown up watching: *The Bill*, *Dangerfield*, *Peak Practice*, *Heartbeat*. More often than not these were just single episodes, so no more than two weeks' work at a time and not a huge amount of money, but they continued to give me experience and fill up my CV.

At the time corporate videos were a really good way to get extra money and still feel as if you were acting. The videos were made by production companies for big businesses. They were usually training films. The scripts would consist of different scenarios that employees may find themselves in and what you should and shouldn't do. I remember playing a doctor's receptionist and I had a load of medical jargon to spew out, which I couldn't quite remember. I taped my lines to my 'keyboard', which was just out of shot, and saved myself from embarrassment! You were given a daily rate for the videos and the more you did the more your rate increased. I remember being paid £250 a day at one point and for a twenty-one-year-old in 1996 that wasn't bad at all.

Of course the work wasn't constant and once the rent and the bills and shopping had been paid it was often a struggle.

Apart from the obvious financial insecurity that being out of work brings, what it also gives you is time. Time to think, to feel, to reflect, to regret, to grieve! You have to have an enormous sense of self-belief and resilience, as months can go by without any work to speak of. I was fairly lucky, I worked as soon as I left drama school, but there were still times where there would be a six-month gap between jobs. I would have to be very disciplined about how I spent my days, including making sure I exercised, which helped me keep on top of my mental health (although I hadn't realized this yet). I didn't always achieve this and there were times when it was really difficult. We're so aware of mental health now and we all know that exercise can be a great stress reliever. When I was twenty-one, I was exercising because I wanted to be good to my body; I hadn't realized how much it helped my head too. But sometimes the struggle of unemployment and the disappointment of losing out on a job meant I let it slide – I couldn't be bothered and I always suffered for it. I would berate myself for having achieved nothing that day. My head would tell me I was lazy and undisciplined. That didn't help, so after a while I learnt that it was easier to just go and exercise.

I was living in Wimbledon, in south-west London, with Marc when I first left drama school. Marc could turn his hand to anything – acting DIY, tech, he was good at all of it! I felt safe, protected, and we lived happily together for six years or so. We were very supportive of each other's careers. This was a time before mobiles, and if we had been out all day the first thing we'd do when we arrived home would be to huddle around the answerphone to see which one of us had a message from our agent. Marc was the first person I knew to have a pager. If something was urgent his agent would page him and he would call them from a phone box while we were out and about. He'd ask me to remember the audition time and date while he memorized the address.

And, when work was quiet, we had each other to lean on. Not working is the hardest thing about my industry. Some people tend to have an idea that actors are working all the time, but the reality is quite different – most of us spend a huge amount of time unemployed. And an average job only lasts three to four months, so we are often thinking about what's next and worrying about the future. Marc and I could talk about that to each other. We shared our fears and frustrations, we motivated each other and financially we could share the load. Rent and bills were always the biggest struggle. I was always trying to make the house look nicer for little to no money and I did a lot of 'upcycling' – at least that's what they call it now! I bought an old table and chairs for next to nothing, painted them bright pink and stapled leopard-print fur on top of the seat pads. I loved all that and Marc would help me if I wasn't able to 'fulfil my visions'!!

I once had an idea that I could make a lampshade out of beads. It was before the internet so I had to go to the bead store in Covent Garden. I picked out what I needed and took them to the cashier. It came to £60! I panicked; I didn't know what to do. I couldn't afford that but I felt too embarrassed to put hundreds of beads back into their little boxes so I handed over my card, sweating. When I got home I cried and told Marc I'd made a mistake, we couldn't afford it, and I would take them all back. He told me to calm down, it was fine, we would be OK and to crack on and just make the thing I'd been so excited about. I did. To say it was a shade that lacked shade would be an understatement. It needed about another 500 beads to get close to being useful but it stayed hung up in our living room until we left. Every time I looked up I would be blinded and think, *That's sixty quid right there!*

Marc and I would talk a lot, we were very open with each other. I would sometimes get upset about Dad but mostly I would suffer from feelings of depression and unworthiness. I can see now that these feelings were unprocessed grief, and the long periods of unemployment meant I had hours of time for my feelings to begin to rise to the surface. However, at this point I was still trying to push them away rather than invite them in and try to understand them – they scared me. I relied on Marc's strength and level-headedness.

Inside, it felt like I was never fully connected to myself. That I was always searching for something. I mistook this for ambition. I would think, *I just need more work, that's all. Work will fix me.* It always did for a time but then I'd come home and feel empty again. Getting the job, the expectation of what was to come, was always really exciting. The prep of costume fittings, read-throughs and schedules were all-consuming. Then the job itself would come along. Whether it was filming for two weeks or touring in theatres for six months, it didn't matter, the end of the job always felt the same. The dread of the silent phone, the rejection sitting side by side with the demand for self-belief. The 'are you working at the moment' question being asked at every party/night out. It all felt like a huge burden. The truth was that, coupled with all these legitimate feelings, there was still a huge amount of grief, waiting patiently for me. The jobs always felt like escapes and subconsciously I knew the return home would be a race between having to face it all or getting another job and running away from everything again. Fear really is a great motivator – until it isn't.

By the time I was twenty-four my drinking had ramped up. Not in frequency but in consequences. Nights would be cut short as I'd have to be taken home by Marc. I'd often just fall asleep somewhere and end up having to stay the night at whoever's house I was at. I always felt terrible the next day. I couldn't work out why I was different to everyone else. Why couldn't I just stop when I'd had enough? I just kept going until I fell asleep.

Everything was catching up with me. The feeling of being untethered kept chasing me around. My life *looked* grounded: a home, partner, friends. My career at this point was really beginning to take shape and work was more frequent and financially rewarding, but the feeling inside didn't match. I was cast in *Coronation Street*, which meant regular money and a little bit of security. Even so, I felt as though I could take off at any minute, like a hot-air balloon detaching itself from its ropes. None of these successes were doing the job of keeping me filled up for long enough.

The tools that I'd been using to drown it out weren't working any more. It's hard to describe but intuitively I knew that the force inside me was more powerful than me. I wouldn't have been able to name it 'grief' at that time, I just knew something was wrong.

The pain I was desperately trying to manage, the problem I was trying to solve, was outwitting me. I couldn't settle. The grief didn't like being ignored and it was becoming noisier. The alcohol was an attempt to drown it out, quieten it down, but it actually made it louder and more forceful. The unprocessed grief that lived like a poison inside me needed something to sit on top of it. To squash and suffocate it. It would take pretty much anything but it needed a lot of it because grief is powerful and it finds a way to peek through the cracks. Essentially I tried to fix my insides on the outside. I hadn't been taught how to attend to my emotional needs and my grief hadn't been processed or handled with the care and attention it so desperately required. The grief had found other places to stay. Places where it could either hide or be my driver. Work, relationships, ambition, my drinking.

And for a while those things had worked. Really well, actually. But at the back of my mind, lurking, waiting for its moment, was always the grief. It was doing press-ups while it was waiting for me. It was getting stronger and more powerful.

By the time I was twenty-six, I started to feel stifled in my relationship with Marc. All of the qualities I'd loved about him I began to reject. His efficiency and the way he handled our lives began to make me feel weak and incapable. It wasn't his fault in any way, I just came to the realization that I relied on him far too heavily, for everything. I needed to grow up and stand on my own two feet, make mistakes and be accountable; I needed to be independent. To face the world on my own.

We separated, and it was so painful – for both of us. But instead of giving myself time alone to learn and grow and ideally begin to see a therapist, I jumped into another relationship. His name was Craig. Sadly for us we were like moths to a flame. I needed to be fixed. I was a bucket of unmet needs. We became very enmeshed almost immediately, relying heavily on each other. I had attached myself to someone. There was love, but also a deep thread of insecurity that made trust and deep connection impossible. I wasn't ready to be in a relationship because we both had so much unravelling and learning to do.

Among the love and devotion and happy times, there was a lot of chaos. I had made the mistake of thinking a different person was what I needed when in fact what needed to change was me.

I first began to see a therapist a year into my relationship with Craig and I was able to offload and talk to her about what was happening inside. I could sense things weren't right. I hadn't been able to connect all the dots yet, but to be listened to and to hear myself out loud was incredibly powerful. I began to realize that my desire to please was costing me the chance of an honest, full life. But, although the therapy was helpful, I don't think I was quite ready to be as honest as I could with her.

There was also a realization beginning to grow inside me. Something disturbing. My life on the outside was looking good. I had really enjoyed my time on *EastEnders* for a couple of years. I played Kate Morton, an undercover cop who tried to frame Phil Mitchell but eventually fell in love with him and married him. Often when you film you get taken to locations and you have no idea where you are. You literally get out of a car, are ushered into a building and then don't leave until it's dark and time to go home. Years later, I moved to Crouch End and, while I was out one day exploring, I stopped outside the town hall. It felt familiar and then it came to me: *How funny, that's where I married Phil.*

After *EastEnders* I'd had the pure joy of winning *Strictly*. I remember being in the green room one day when Christopher Parker, who played Spencer Moon, came bundling in. I always loved him and his energy. He told me he'd taken part in this brand-new show called *Strictly Come Dancing* and did I want to watch a bit of it. 'Of course I do,' I said as he popped in the VHS and we watched on the communal telly. I was transfixed. *This looks like so much fun*, I thought. Less than a year later I was being approached by the lovely Sharon Hanley, who was head of publicity at the time, asking if I'd be interested. I gave myself a night to think about it but I knew I was going to say yes. I ADORED *Strictly* from start to finish. It really was all-consuming. It was new and challenging and nerve-racking and I was moving my body every day. It felt amazing! I couldn't wait to get to rehearsals each day and my dance partner Darren Bennett easily matched my enthusiasm. He worked me really hard and it was intense and incredibly exciting. I will never forget how alive I felt throughout that whole process (and terrified . . . even now the music makes my stomach churn!!!).

Immediately after *Strictly* I was cast as Roxie Hart in *Chicago*, my first lead in a West End show. I owned my own home by this point and I felt really proud of being able to make a good living doing what I loved. I was still very ambitious with regards to my career and there were many things I wanted to achieve, but that wasn't it. The realization was that the emptiness – the inability to sustain satisfaction, the disconnection I had felt for so long – was still very, very prevalent. It hadn't gone anywhere. So, although the thoughts of *I'll feel better when I have my own home, I just need some financial stability* and *If I was married, it would be different* were all coming true, they weren't 'fixing' me. I still felt lost.

Chapter 4

The birth of Harvey

———

I was confused; I thought something was wrong with me. But it was all about to become very clear. I decided it was time to confront my relationship with alcohol.

Craig and I were together for six years. We were married after five and a year after that had our baby boy, Harvey, who is by far the best thing that's ever happened to me. I'd always wanted to be a mam and Harvey was very much planned. When we found out we were expecting, we were elated. I had always said I wanted three children. The idea of being a big family, a gang, really appealed to me. Sadly for myself and Craig, it didn't work out like that and we divorced before Harvey was two.

Children are the great leveller. All the things I wasn't able to ask for or feel I deserved for myself changed once Harvey was born. It was easy for me to see what my son needed. That was simple and clear. What he didn't need was two parents whose arguing and misalignment were more prevalent than ever. After all the pain and miscommunication, we divorced knowing it was the right thing to do. Craig is now happy with his partner and we have a fantastic co-parenting relationship.

After Craig, I began a new relationship that lasted a couple of years. He was an actor; kind, handsome and driven. His name was Paul. He was a very positive person and I loved his outlook on life. We made the most of our time together and he was excellent with Harvey, who was one when we first met.

We met in 2009 when we were both working on the West End musical *Legally Blonde*. You learn something profound about yourself from each and every partner, and this relationship showed me just how much work I had to do in order to allow myself to be loved. I wouldn't have been able to name this at the time but I hadn't even begun my journey of truly looking inward. I was still looking outwards. I still continued to place other people's feelings about me above my feelings towards them. This was my pattern. I was fragile and hurt and I allowed the relationship to distract me so I could avoid the internal work I so desperately needed to do. I'd be so intent on getting them to love me I'd forget about my own feelings. All I needed to do was make sure they never wanted to leave me. Again, exhausting and entirely unfair for both sides.

I was LOVING *Legally Blonde*. The show was a huge hit and the cast and crew were awesome. I was living in Covent Garden and Harvey attended a nursery in Soho. I'd separated from Craig a couple of months after the show opened, so I was unbelievably tired; the emotional turmoil paired with the physical exhaustion of the show was a lot to deal with. I had employed an evening nanny to look after Harvey while I did the show. Her name was Natalia and she was a dream, but the first time I left Harvey he screamed so badly. I remember calling my mam as I walked to the theatre on the Strand.

'I can't do it. I can't do the show. I feel terrible. Harvey is screaming.'

Mam calmed me down and told me that it would only take a week or so before Harvey felt comfortable. She was right. The months rolled by. I would perform in the evening and then rush home to get to bed as I knew Harvey would wake early. On the day I had two shows I had to take Harvey to nursery, go to the theatre, perform the show and then run as fast as I could back to Soho before the nursery closed. It would then be back to Covent Garden to feed and bathe Harvey, wait for Natalia to arrive and then go back to the Savoy for an evening show. I was exhausted. I worked out that there was a twenty-five-minute gap between my exit from Act One and my first entrance for Act Two. I would ask Paul to knock on my dressing-room door before he went down for his first Act Two number, 'Whipped into Shape'. This meant I could catch a little nap and then have time to fix my make-up and wig before I went back on.

My relationship with Paul really highlighted my drinking. I was beginning to remove things from my life, which was allowing me to see more clearly. I started to realize that alcohol was really holding me back.

It was New Year's Eve. I'd left *Legally Blonde* by this time but Paul was still performing in it. I was celebrating at a friend's house in Newcastle and Paul was driving up straight after the matinee. He expected to arrive before midnight. I told him to call me when he was near and I would give him the full post-code. I got really drunk, really quick, forgot to check my phone and left Paul having to call my mam to ask if she knew where I was. Fortunately she did and was able to give him the info.

I don't remember Paul turning up, but I do remember how hurt he was the next day – and rightly so. I felt terrible; the lack of care and thought after he had travelled all that way didn't align with who I was. This was the most confusing part for me. I would behave in a way that didn't match up with my values. I began to see that I became a different person when I drank and I didn't always like who I became. I needed to be honest with myself and the people in my life. The relationship wasn't what I wanted and I felt I was going to make both of us very unhappy. It ended and I was finally on my own.

Despite this confusion I did have a pretty good grasp on who I was and what my values were. I knew I was a good person. I had made mistakes and had regrets but at the heart of it my intentions were always good. But something was wrong. Something still didn't feel right. I had removed the relationships and the fight to be loved that came with them. I was on my own with my son. I was free to be whatever I wanted to be. It was my time to fly. But I couldn't.

The word *grief* comes from the Latin and French meaning heavy. That was how I felt: stuck, and heavy.

For a long time, alcohol had helped me escape: to stop thinking, to change the way I felt about myself. Conversely, I thought it also helped me access all the things that lay dormant inside me. I felt connected with alcohol, as if I could communicate more deeply and truthfully, when in fact I was just masking my feelings by yet again putting something on top of them. Yes, it was sometimes fun and it definitely wasn't all bad, not by a long shot, but the bad feelings after a night out started to outweigh any of the goodness I was receiving.

I think it might be important to stress here how I drank at this point, because we all have such different relationships to alcohol. I was still a social drinker, which meant I never drank alone and it was almost always on nights out. It wouldn't be done around Harvey but what he would be on the receiving end of was a mother who was distracted or feeling anxious as a result of one of those nights out. Afterwards I would go weeks without drinking and in between those times I would be consciously looking after myself. I say this because my alcoholism was very much about the *way* I drank as opposed to the frequency of my drinking. It also wasn't *every* time I went out. That is why it took me a while to admit I needed help. If I didn't drink all the time and I sometimes drank safely then how could I have a problem? All I knew was that it rarely made me happy any more. Whether that unhappiness was because of something I did or said during those nights out, or simply the way I felt for the next few days as the alcohol left my body, started to matter less to me. The events became less relevant and the feelings became magnified. It was hard to ignore. Alcohol didn't agree with me and for some reason my relationship with it and the way I used it desperately needed to be looked at. I had been unable to connect the dots and see the link. I was confused; I thought something was wrong with me, but it was all about to become very clear. I decided it was time to confront my relationship with alcohol.

In March 2013, I headed to an AA meeting in central London. I felt a mix of shame and desperation as I approached the door. I was greeted by a friendly man who smiled and said, 'Good afternoon, welcome.' The room was in a basement but still had light coming through the small windows at street level. The chairs filled the room and it already looked full despite the meeting not being due to start for another ten minutes. I took a seat at the back and attempted to take it all in. As I calmed myself down I noticed a woman walking around the room asking a few of the attendees if they would be happy to do a reading. She looked radiant, happy. *I want what she has!* I thought. I took a closer look and realized I recognized her; she was an actress, and I immediately felt as if I'd come to the right place. She looked at me and smiled warmly. I wanted to cry so bad. The meeting began and I experienced something I never have before. People, strangers, sharing how they feel. No small talk or pretence, just real, authentic feelings.

They were talking about how their insides didn't match their outsides, how they struggled with feelings of unworthiness, and for the first time in my life I felt completely seen. I was under no illusion that it would be a long journey and there was work to be done, but I felt safe and I felt positive, as if I'd done something really caring for myself.

A few weeks and several more meetings later, and I know that I am definitely in the right place. I say the words for the first time. I have been reluctant so far. I don't want to admit defeat (oh, the irony). I AM defeated, I am lost, but I am humble enough and desperate enough to accept a different way, and so I say, 'My name is Jill and I'm an alcoholic.'

I'm relieved. I feel a weight lift from my shoulders and the 'coat I wear' feels a little lighter.

That was more than eleven years ago, and I have never looked back.

My belief (and it's very personal to me) is that my constant pushing away of grief became so intolerable that alcohol was the only release I had. The loss I had experienced after losing Dad had never been attended to. It had been ignored and it had mutated into all sorts of behaviours. Some of which served me really well – my strength and determination, my empathy, my work ethic. They were all great qualities, but the problem was the engine they were being driven with.

The pressure valve had finally burst and it was a great relief to me to know that I could stop and alleviate the suffering by sharing and communicating with others.

The next two years were a revelation. A truly transformative period where I stepped into myself and became a woman and mother that I felt really proud of being. I started looking at my grief in a way that I never had before. I gave it time and energy and I treated it with care and tenderness.

I started to try to understand our family dynamics and the choices I'd made. I began to have sympathy for myself. I had believed life was a fight, and I needed to be in the ring at all times. I had exhausted myself. I started to ease off and gain a wider perspective. Things began to make a bit more sense, and with the alcohol removed I could see all of me. I could see that my defensiveness was a barrier to my real vulnerability, my people-pleasing was fear of abandonment, my low self-esteem a symptom of my alcoholism most likely brought on by my unmet needs. The early years of my life when the grief for my dad wasn't attended to meant that I had tried to make up for it myself. I realized that the small girl inside of me had grown up too fast. She had overridden all her own circuitry in pursuit of external validation and she needed to go back and find out who she was.

Some friends and family found it difficult. Who was sober Jill? I didn't laugh as hard at their jokes, I didn't make myself the clown for their amusement, and maybe my sobriety held up a mirror to some of the things they didn't like so much about themselves. I don't know. All I do know is it's an interesting dynamic. I realized that a lot of the things I 'enjoyed' were only enjoyable *because* of the booze. I actually don't really like clubbing. I did it because everyone else was and I didn't want to be boring. I also realized how boring most drunk people are (and, yes, I include myself in that). The banal chat and finding ourselves soooooo much funnier than we actually are was an amusing lesson to learn, especially when I reflected back (and cringed).

I started to meet mates for lunch or breakfast. It was such a tonic to see them at the beginning of the day, before they were stressed or run down by whatever was thrown at them later on. Some friendships fell by the wayside but others only strengthened and grew. In recovery, I was blown away to find that other alcoholics would happily give up their time to sit and chat with me for no other reason than connection – the thing all alcoholics are searching for. It's what we were all given when we joined, and the idea is that you keep on giving back what you received so the circle never breaks.

Once, about a year after my first meeting, I was having a really bad day. I was in a meeting in north London and I was feeling hopeless and panicking that maybe I was doing it all wrong. I shared where I was and, as usual, people listened until my time was up. At the end, a lady asked me if I wanted to go for a coffee. She took me to a Café Rouge and she listened and she sympathized and she identified. I was so struck by her kindness. It was a Sunday evening, she didn't have to do any of this, but she was simply giving back what had been given to her when she first arrived. The kindness I have witnessed in the rooms of AA is so touching. The simplicity of giving someone your time and attention is the greatest gift.

I was thawing out and I could feel the softening. Sometimes it was frightening to be so raw and vulnerable but I was ready to keep on peeling back the layers. I was beginning to see what I really wanted versus what I thought I wanted. The armour was being dropped and I was enjoying not having to add to myself to make me more interesting, attractive, successful. I was attempting to remove the onion layers so I could hear and see the real me for the first time in a long time.

It still amazes me, eleven years later, that removing something from my life could reveal so much. I can honestly say that putting down the alcohol meant there was room and reflection for the deep, deep grief that was about to start enveloping me. My sober journey meant I could look myself in the eye and feel complete sympathy for the girl who had smothered her feelings down and didn't make room for her wants or needs. It's helped me understand why I had felt so alone for so long regardless of whether I was in a relationship or not. I had confused being able to talk about my feelings with feeling my feelings.

There's a saying in 12-step recovery: 'The good news is you get your feelings back . . . the bad news is you get your feelings back.' I slowly began to trust myself. To appreciate how far I had come in my life and how much I'd achieved despite all of the struggle. As I settled into myself and my body, I could meet people in a way that felt much more authentic; I learnt what it was like to develop relationships that were honest and without conditions.

Two years passed and I felt hopeful about the future. I could see what I had to offer and I felt positive. That was when Matt came into my life . . .

Chapter 5

Matt

We jump in the car and all I can think is *YES*. In big, illuminated letters. YES.

It's the middle of 2014, I've been sober for just over a year and I'm feeling the best I've felt for a long time. I'm filming *Babylon* for Channel 4. It's being directed by Danny Boyle and I'm so excited to be working with him. Jesse Armstrong and Sam Bain have created the series and I'm filming with a cast including now-Oscar winner Daniel Kaluuya. The whole team is fantastic and we have a really good time on set. The show is set in London and I'm playing Davina, a member of the Territorial Support Group. Life feels good.

I feel ready to have someone special in my life. I'm living in Crouch End, London. Harvey is six and enjoying school. Myself and his dad are in a really good place, we are co-parenting and things feel hopeful. We have a system where we have decided to do week on, week off. That way Harvey gets to spend some decent time with each of us and not feel as if he's back and forth too much. Our communication feels good and if one of us is working (Craig is also an actor) the other takes the slack.

I have a friend who lives close by. Her name is Polly and she's a friend I made later on in my life. We were both thirty-four when we met. I was doing *Legally Blonde* at the Savoy Theatre and in the middle of a divorce, and so although I was loving the job, I was very stressed personally. We were introduced on the set of a show called *Angela and Friends*, hired to be talking heads, the same format as *Loose Women*. We were paid to have opinions and we didn't struggle! She was a journalist – petite, funny, with a dyed red bob – and we bonded one day in the make-up room over a very specific moment in an episode of Katie Price and Peter Andre's *Katie and Peter: The Next Chapter*. We laughed at the fact we even watched the show, let alone cared about the content. I knew I wanted her in my life and that she was special. Little did I know then what an important part of my life she would become.

Polly, unbeknown to me, has asked her friend Jim if he knows of any men who he thinks I'd like. Matt is mentioned and Polly and I immediately try to find any evidence of him on the internet. We come across a grainy video of him being interviewed about his business, a dating website. He seems nice, handsome. Jim says he'll make an introduction.

It's six months later and nothing has happened. Jim is distracted; his partner Jordan (also my friend) is pregnant with their first child and they are buying a house. I can't possibly ask them to sort out my love life as well, so I take matters into my own hands and I join Matt's website!

I know, I know, why didn't I just ask Jim for Matt's number? It seems ridiculous now, but there you go. I join using a pseudonym. I had never used a dating site before, but that's what people tell me they do. 'Oh no, don't use your own name!' So I use Colette, my confirmation name from when I was thirteen, chosen because there was a girl in my school called Colette who was really pretty and lovely and not because I admired St Colette!

I tell Polly what I have done, and she thinks I'm ridiculous (fair). She gives Jim another nudge and numbers are exchanged.

It's a day or so later, so I've not thought about the number exchange too much. I'm in a taxi, heading into the countryside just outside London to a yoga retreat. I first started yoga at drama school. Our movement teacher Ed would take a daily class and I loved it. More recently I've joined a local studio and have been doing hot yoga almost every day. It makes me feel really alive and it's helping me calm down my system because I have to focus so much on my breath and finding space in my body. It's my new 'thing'. I've made some friends at the studio and I'm looking forward to a weekend of good chats and nourishing food and exercise.

My phone signal is getting worse the further out into the country we go, but I hear a beep and notice there is a message on my phone. It's Matt. He's introducing himself and wondering if I fancy a chat. His voice sounds so good, gentle yet confident. I decide to call him when I get there, but when I arrive the signal is still bad. So I go to the top floor of the stately home and I stick my head out of the attic room window. It's the only place my phone works. He thinks it's hilarious that I joined his dating site in order to try to somehow meet him. We continue chatting for the next week and we decide to go on a date.

It's a week or so later and the morning of our first date (just my second in two years). I'm excited and nervous. We are meeting at one, which is perfect as it gives time for my face to de-puff (an exciting new development of ageing!). I spend too much time wondering what to wear but decide on a red and black jumper, jeans and a parka. I want to look like I haven't tried when actually it's taken me three hours to perfect the natural look. My phone beeps; it's a text from him. *Oh god*, I think, *please don't cancel or say you're gonna be late. That'll really piss me off.* The text reads: *Il neige.*

What the fuck is that! Is he deliberately being obtuse because he's got cold feet and wants to cancel? I don't know how to answer. I can't ask what it means, he might think I'm stupid. I google it. It's French and it means 'It's snowing.' FFS why didn't he just say that? I panic. Maybe he isn't right for me. Maybe we are just very different people and we won't gel. I'm overthinking massively. Five minutes later the doorbell rings; my stomach is churning as I open the door. He has his back to me and he does a kind of Richard Curtis turn to camera as he looks to me and smiles. 'Hello.'

I smile. 'Hello.' His hair is silver grey, his smile is wide and his blue eyes sparkle. He's wearing a teal chunky-knit jumper, jeans and boots. I don't know what it is about great knitwear on men but the 'handsome fisherman look' really does it for me. We jump in the car and all I can think is *YES*. In big, illuminated letters. YES. (Weeks later I will go to his flat and above the fireplace will be a huge red poster with a lightbulb on it. Inside, the bulb will read YES!)

Today we walk in the countryside; it's a perfect wintry afternoon, crisp yet sunny. We talk and talk. We discuss family, past relationships, passions. We hold hands, he worries my boots will get too muddy, he asks me what superpower I would have if I could choose only one. Invisibility, I say. He says he would also choose that but he'd asked his sister the same question and she had said healing hands. After her beautiful answer he said he felt shallow. I said it was a beautiful answer but I'd still wanna be invisible!

We stop at a pub for a drink and then head back to Crouch End. I ask him if he would like to order pizza and come back to mine. He laughs and says he had the exact same thought. We eat pizza back at mine and I introduce him to Patti Stanger on *Millionaire Matchmaker*. It's a dating show in America for millionaires. Patti is hilarious and so is the show. It's cheesy and I love it. Matt is in immediately. It's perfect and so is he.

Three months later and we are in love and feel sure we have a future together. He's smart, handsome, interesting and funny. He has an intoxicating mix of eccentricity and realness. He wanders around his flat in bright orange felt slippers that look like clogs, he drives miles out of his way to get the perfect pastel de nata but also has the ability to know if someone in a room needs his help or attention.

Once we start dating, it progresses pretty fast. To say we feel drawn to each other would be an understatement. Everything feels right, which isn't to say it's all easy, but it's worth it. He's a worrier; so am I, but I suppress my own stuff to try to buoy him up. He's feeling at a crossroads with work and we talk about it endlessly. I want so much to be able to help but I know that ultimately he's an entrepreneur and he will have to find a road he's happy with.

Within a year, we've moved in together. We planned to buy a house while trying for a baby and to get married (in that order), but at this point we are renting a flat that we picked out together and we are looking for potential properties to buy. It's great to be living together. Matt is wondering what his next venture will be. He is doing some freelance work while also writing a book and we love being able to wake up and go to bed with each other every day. It feels exciting. We often say that we wish we could have met each other sooner but I know that we have met at the perfect time, because now we are ready for each other.

Harvey and Matt were developing a really beautiful relationship, but there was an occasion early on that surprised me, to say the least. We had decided to go to central London, to a pub we had heard did great Sunday roasts. Matt was a total foodie and would constantly be seeking out the best places to eat. After dinner we all decided that we had room for pudding. All three of us went for sticky toffee. Matt and I polished ours off no problem, but Harvey struggled, and stopped halfway through.

'You not gonna eat that?' asked Matt.

'I'm full,' came the answer from Harvey.

'Can I have it, then?' Matt said.

Harvey looked at him and then he locked eyes with me as he ever so slowly spat into the remains of the pudding. It was an act of pure defiance that I'd never seen from him before. I was so mad – and intrigued. Matt went red and I told Harvey off. It was a perfect display of 'You've taken my mam, you ain't gonna take my pudding.'

I understand: kids don't get a choice when someone new comes into their lives. Matt didn't have any children of his own and it was a big deal for both of them to meet each other.

You'll be pleased to know they went on to share many puds together. And as their relationship developed they evolved their own rituals and jokes. When Matt arrived home from work, he and Harvey would huddle underneath a blanket on the sofa and have boy chat. I loved watching them develop their own dynamic. Blending a family is hard and takes time and patience. Harvey would love to tell Matt that his dad was funnier than him. He also liked to tell him that his dad was taller than him. He wasn't – not even close – but Matt and I would laugh at the beautiful innocence and loyalty of it all.

As our relationship progressed and the intimacy evolved, Matt would sometimes mention dying to me. I listened, but I didn't like it; it really upset me. It felt very real. Very much like some kind of premonition. It also scared me, because I knew at my core that we don't know what's in store for us. I had experienced how life can change irrevocably in one moment. Without any warning Dad had gone, vanished, never to be seen again. Once you have experienced this it's hard not to panic and think it might happen to someone else you love. But I had to hold on to the idea that although terrible things do happen, so do amazing things. Every single day, amazing beautiful things happen. Matt knew all about my dad and he knew, more than anyone I've ever met, how precious life was.

One night we had been chatting and kissing on the sofa. I got up to get something from the kitchen, but he pulled me back in. He had an intense look in his eyes and he said to me with complete earnestness, 'Jill, if I die, promise me you will meet someone else and find love again.'

I wish I could tell you that I hugged him tightly and reassured him. Instead, my stomach dropped. I felt like he knew something I didn't. It also felt eerily similar to a conversation my mam and dad had had before he died, and I couldn't allow that to happen. My mam had told me she had been chatting in bed with Dad three days before he passed. He asked her what she would do if he was ever to die. Mam said, 'I would marry your Derek, he's lonely and he's a nice man.' 'Yeah, that would be nice,' Dad had replied.

I looked at Matt, frightened, and with a panic rising as my stomach tightened.

'What are you saying that for? Please don't say things like that. You're not going anywhere and neither am I.'

He didn't answer but he looked as scared as me.

That really disturbed me – it felt way too foreboding. Looking back, maybe he did feel something. Maybe he did know. Matt did something from the very beginning of our relationship that annoyed and delighted me in equal measure. He would always ask me for five more minutes . . .

If we were cuddling on the sofa and I moved to get up, he would say, 'Five more minutes.'

If we were in bed and I tried to get up to go for a shower, he would ask, 'Five more minutes.'

If we were in a coffee shop eating pastries and chatting and I moved to leave: 'Five more minutes.'

It always felt as though he had a different awareness of time from me. That he knew how precious the simplest of moments were.

Tuesday, 18 January 2017. Matt wakes early to leave for a spin class.

To say he was a noisy man would be like saying mammoths are a bit hairy. That man could create noise with a spoon and a bowl of cereal that would wake up even the deepest of sleepers. Needless to say I wake up too and decide to go to the loo. It's 7.15 and the class begins in fifteen minutes. He was always late, always. I shuffle past him in the kitchen and off I go to the loo. We're using an ovulation kit and the first pee of the day is the most reliable, apparently. So, with eyes half open, I pee on the stick and wait to see what's happening. I look up and Matt's at the door. We're not in the habit of following each other to the toilet but he's leaning against the doorway looking at me with a very peaceful and loving gaze. I feel a little embarrassed being on the loo but the look in his eyes reassures me and I relax. As I stare at him, he begins to look pixelated. *How strange*, I think. *It looks like he's fading away.* I put it down to being really tired. He leaves the doorway, I shuffle back into the kitchen, kiss him and tell him I love him.

About forty-five minutes later, having gone back to sleep, I'm awoken by a knock at the door. The knock becomes louder and I go to the door with a sense that something bad has happened. A man who I've never seen before asks me if I am Matt's partner. He tells me he works at the gym and Matt has had an accident. I ask him what exactly has happened and all he can say is: 'Please come to the gym.' I wouldn't be able to describe him to you, I couldn't detail one single feature on his face, but what I can tell you is his eyes looked pleading and scared – very, very scared. He needs me to come with him. I go back to the bedroom, quickly throw on some clothes and pick up my phone.

Seventeen missed calls. This must be bad.

I run to the gym with the young man. A million thoughts race through my mind: Maybe he's broken his back. Yeah, a back break would be really bad. Loads of recovery time and possible ramifications. What if it's his neck? He could be paralysed. What will I tell him if he's paralysed?

I arrive at the gym. It's a basement studio and I'm a member so I know exactly what room the class is in. I rush down the stairs but a paramedic stops me from going in. The look on his face is grave. It tells me everything I need to know.

'Is he dead?' I hear myself say.

'Not yet,' he replies.

The air leaves my body and my legs feel totally incapable of holding me up. I slip slowly to the floor and try to breathe while on all fours. It's hard to explain how the news feels. The idea that the man I love, who was staring at me an hour ago, is potentially dead, is impossible to comprehend and yet my body does just that. My body knew what was being said and it decides it needs to be as low to the ground as possible. To be steadied, anchored. After a few minutes I'm allowed into the room. Matt is lying on the floor of the studio, his eyes half open.

'Matt, Matt,' I cry. 'It's me, I'm here.'

His eyes flicker as if he knows I'm with him now, and then they close, never to open again. I watch as they use the defibrillator but there's no response. I look at his feet; he's wearing spin shoes. They're hard and tight-fitting and I want to remove them. To make him comfortable. Matt loves being comfortable. He's never happier than in a kaftan and flip-flops. Much to the piss-taking of his friends. He doesn't care, he loves a Dish-Dash and we all love him for it.

It's decided he has to go immediately to the nearest hospital, in Hampstead. Matt is six foot. It's apparent, lying flat out on a stretcher, he won't fit in the lift, so the two paramedics and I carry him up the staircase. As we do, I stare at the stairs. The lyrics of 'I'm Still Standing' are written on them. Since I won *Strictly Come Dancing* in 2009, the song has followed me around. People tell me when they hear it they think of me dancing the jive. But now, as I carry Matt, the words suddenly take on a different meaning. We get to the top of the stairs and out of the building and while the paramedics put Matt into the ambulance I call the only person I want to speak to, my mam.

'I'm getting on a train now,' she says.

'Mam, I think I've lost him.'

'No,' she says, 'don't say that.'

But the truth is by this time I understand how long Matt's been without oxygen. How many failed resuscitations there have been and how long it's been from his heart attack to now. We're blue-lighted to the hospital as I watch more failed attempts with the defibrillator from the back of the ambulance. It's a horror show. As soon as we arrive he's hooked up to machines, and he looks calm again. I ask them to remove his shoes.

The next twenty-four hours are a blur of tears, family, friends, shock and utter disbelief. No one can comprehend what is happening. He's pronounced dead the next day.

I call Harvey from the hospital. There is no way I'm going to lie to him or tell him a half truth. I can't have him confused or left out as I was.

I explain Matt has had an accident at the gym and he has died. I say I'm very, very sad but it's going to be OK. I need him to know the truth but also to know that there is a way through this. I keep it simple and direct. I don't talk about angels or heaven. That's for him to decide. All I need him to know is that Matt is dead and although it's devastating we will survive it. The call doesn't last long but it's clear and he knows he can call me if he needs to know anything else.

And that's when it all begins. The long, painful journey through grief again.

I knew I had to do this differently. I couldn't repeat history. The years of unravelling and all the work I had done to get me back to feeling like me again were not going to be in vain. I was going to face the pain and let my body and my head experience all it needed to process what had happened. In the first few weeks after Matt's death, Dad's death hit me again. Now the gates are open, I have to let it all in. I'm scared. Really, really scared.

Chapter 6

Matt's dead, Matt's dead, Matt's dead

———

Where are you? Have you left me altogether? Why can't I dream of you?

Time moves slowly in grief but those first few weeks were torturous. Every night I'd dread sleep. I would wake up crying. My body would spasm and feel like it was fitting. I was finding loud noises extremely upsetting, and any siren, but especially ambulances, would make my heart race. Matt's body on the spin studio floor, carrying him up the studio stairs, watching them trying to resuscitate him in the ambulance were all images that would swirl around my head. They were becoming more and more intrusive and difficult to keep at bay.

God knows how much cortisol my body had running through it. I knew it needed to calm down and recalibrate. No one had diagnosed me and I didn't go to my doctor; I didn't want to be medicated. I knew enough to understand that I was suffering from PTSD. It was hardly surprising.

I made myself a promise very early on that I was going to walk straight through the centre of my grief. No shortcuts and definitely no avoidance. I needed to do what I had not been able to with Dad. I wanted to feel it all.

Of course there is no perfect way to grieve and I faltered many, many times, believing I couldn't do it. I longed to put it away and save it for another day/week /year, but I felt for me this would only prolong the recovery. Each time I fell I managed to get back up and remind myself that the pain wouldn't kill me.

I recently looked back at some of my diary entries from around that time.

Wed 8 March 2017

Terrible day, hit me like a tsunami. Where are you? Have you left me altogether? Why can't I dream of you? Are there others who need you more? How? I feel hostile, moody, angry, fiery, weak, tired. My face . . . who am I? Puffy, old, saggy. Want to abandon myself. Please bring me back to myself. Too much, everyone is too much and no one is too little. Fuckin torture, why me? Why my life?

It's painful to read back but I think it's important to share. The intensity and brutality of the feelings are hard to communicate with another person. It's difficult to be that honest with someone else so I wanted to show you that I have been there too. The loneliness of grief is the sense that you cannot dare say out loud how you really feel for fear of people either rejecting you or being repulsed by you.

One of the most difficult things was waking. I would usually fall asleep as the sun was rising, having spent a night of insomnia wondering how I was going to cope. The night would consist of crying, but not too loud as I didn't want to wake Harvey; I was feeling incredibly anxious about my son and what effect I was having on him. I was experiencing terrible feelings of hopelessness; every night felt like a dark night of the soul. I would torture myself with the whys: Did I do something wrong? Was it my fault? I introduced him to the gym! Am I being punished? Shall I drink? Will I ever feel OK?!!!! Around and around I'd go. A merry-go-round of punishing thoughts. There was no way I could have slept – the stillness of the night meant the voices in my head were loud. So I could fall asleep only as the sun rose and the noise of the day began.

As the alarm went off, I would open my eyes and for the tiniest moment I would have forgotten what happened. For just a small second Matt was in bed with me and I was about to say good morning. And then I'd remember. And it crushed me all over again. It was horrendous.

So now I hated going to sleep AND waking up.

As a little girl I had suffered from nightmares. I would wake up screaming, convinced there were snakes in my bed. My mam would pull back the duvet to prove there was nothing there. I was afraid to sleep because I didn't want to go through the trauma of the night terrors. The nightmares were clearly unprocessed trauma and no doubt related to Dad but I never connected the two at the time. Maybe my mam never made that connection herself? If only we could have talked about Dad more, then maybe the 'big terrible thing' would go away. The snakes would leave because they weren't in the dark any more. I explained to mam that I was afraid to close my eyes in case I had a nightmare.

One evening, she said to me, 'Before you go to sleep let the last thing you say to yourself be . . . "I don't want to dream."'

'Will that work?' I asked.

And in the way only mams can, she looked at me and said with complete assurance, 'Yes.'

And I believed her.

Obviously I had to somewhat complicate matters – I decided it had to be the very, very absolute last thought in my head before I slept. So, if I said it and then had any other thought whatsoever, I would have to repeat the mantra again. This could sometimes mean I was saying 'I don't want to dream' upward of thirty times a night. But it worked! And it honestly felt like a superpower, like I had conquered my nemesis.

So, after Matt died, I decided I couldn't cope with having to re-remember his death every morning; I would train myself to repeat a mantra the minute I awoke. It had worked when I was a kid so why wouldn't it now? My mantra was: Matt's dead, Matt's dead, Matt's dead. I had learnt to use the power of saying something out loud to control my feelings.

Even writing it now makes me feel sad. The things we do to cope – but it seemed to me that it was way more painful to have even a fleeting moment of thinking he was alive than it was to repeat my macabre mantra each morning.

A few weeks after Matt's death, the days had become full of organization and planning. Choosing venues, speaking to celebrants. I felt largely out of my body. I was observing what was happening but couldn't quite connect to it being my life.

I woke on the morning of his cremation. I just needed this day to be over. The dread that filled my system was overwhelming and I wanted to run away, far away for ever. I sat at the front of the crematorium and stared at the huge coffin, which was yellow, his favourite colour. I could not and did not want to believe he was inside. HE wasn't. I watched the essence of who he was leave his body at the hospital. As his body broke down his spirit left. By the time I asked the nurse to remove his oxygen mask so I could give him one last kiss I knew he was there in body only.

My eulogy was a thank-you, to Matt, thanking him for all the wonderful things he brought into my life and for all those extra five minutes. In writing it I had an enormous sense of gratitude for what he had given me. I experienced a real moment of grace and humility and even though it was going to be torturous without him I knew then that he had made an indelible mark on me, for which I was truly grateful. I wanted people to hear Matt in my eulogy, the whole person, not just the good bits! I often find eulogies perfunctory and full of platitudes. I wanted his friends and family to *feel* him with us. I told them how he would drive me mad *and* make my heart sing. I wanted him to live again. For everyone to feel his presence and energy. And in that moment, he WAS there. We were together and he was so present and alive.

Harvey was at the funeral too. He sat with me for a while at the front and then returned to his dad, who was standing at the back. The room was packed and full of love.

I predicted that there would be a huge crash waiting for me after the wake and there was.

My journey through grief was only just beginning and it was to bring me lessons (both welcome and unwelcome), huge discoveries about myself and a tsunami of emotions that would sweep me off my feet when I was least expecting it.

Chapter 7

Friends

The anxiety of socializing as a griever is
difficult to describe . . . It felt as though
people were either avoiding me or looking at
me with pity. It was all going on in my head.

March 2017

Worried people are gonna start expecting me to get better. I won't. I'm getting worse, much, much worse. The unbearable pain is increasing as the days go by. Had a terrible day yesterday. So, so lonely being a single Mum. With Harv yesterday and kept bursting out crying. Poor, poor Harvey, love him so much.

I really hate parks, they make me feel so lonely. Terribly lonely. I'm so fuckin angry. Very sad and incredibly down. I'm feeling panicked, I will be losing my family and friends because I will be the most miserable friend they have ever had. If people try to cheer me up, I will be so angry.

The flat is filled with cards, my phone beeps constantly with messages from people who have heard the news. Some want it confirmed because they have read it on social media, others tell me how sorry and shocked they are. They ask if they can come over, help, if I need anything, if there is anything at all they can do, but the truth is I just don't have the bandwidth to deal with it. Too many questions! I am both comforted by the attention and repulsed by it.

The living room is full of beautiful flowers but I know why they are there and when they die and the water begins to smell I will have to get rid of each one and it will be a reminder that

Matt too has died. The constant contact and 'I'm sorry for your loss' messages don't touch the sides. I need sustenance and depth; I'm drowning and I need air.

Polly, my dear friend who lives nearby, arranges for me to talk to her aunt Mary, the kind of woman who you think only exists in fairy tales because you can't believe there is someone out there so kind and so very wise. Aunt Mary has suffered many losses in her life and is well aware that life is fleeting. She sits opposite me at Polly's kitchen table and she listens. I tell her I'm bereft, I'm furious, I'm raging! She nods. 'Yes, of course,' she says.

'But I'm going to walk THROUGH it,' I say. 'I'm not going to let it kill me.'

'No, you won't,' she replies. Mary doesn't flinch as I pour out my heart and lay my feelings bare on the table. She listens, she smiles (because she relates) and she never tries to fix or save me. She shares back about losing her husband and how he lives within her. I feel less mad. Mary is neither shocked nor repulsed nor surprised by me. She *knows* humanity in all its forms and she has stood face to face with grief many times.

She makes me feel like it's gonna be OK.

The weeks go by and my family and very close friends stay connected. The emotions are still raw and they are still feeling the ripple effects. It's not hard for them to imagine how I'm feeling so it's not difficult for me to talk to them.

More weeks go by and life picks up pace. The contact dies down and people go back to their lives. There are a few people who I speak to daily, without fail. They are my rocks. Phone calls from others become less frequent. When they do call, it seems like there is a bigger gap between us. I feel as though they feel uncomfortable now; they are willing me to be better but most of the time I feel worse. The shock has worn off and the reality is setting in. It brings with it a deep depression and immense anxiety for the future. The main question being: 'Will I ever feel truly happy again?'

I thought as time moved on I would feel better, less raw. Turns out I just miss Matt more.

I remember, in the first few weeks after Matt died, being furious with complete strangers. If I passed a cafe or a bus stop and heard people laughing I would be so offended. How could they be happy when something so terrible had happened? (I am reminded of my mam at Dad's funeral.) This is the great conflict with grief. Your friends have lives and they have every right to get on with them and to be happy; it doesn't mean they can't be holding you in their heart. Just because they don't feel the same pain as you doesn't mean they don't care. But it's wise to choose who we surround ourselves with very carefully. In those early stages of loss we are all so vulnerable.

At many points I felt like a newborn baby. I can remember walking Harvey to school and thinking that I'd never noticed the path looking that way before. I was holding *his* hand but in many ways I felt like he was walking me. The world looked different.

Colours, shapes, smells, all unfamiliar. It feels like the world has changed and my brain has not been given time to catch up. Small simple tasks become overwhelming and difficult.

I had already been seeing a therapist for a year or so before Matt's death. Her name was Madeline and she had been amazing in the time we had already spent together. My sister and Mam knew how much I had connected with her. One particularly bad day, my anxiety was weighing me down and I was struggling to stop crying. They both suggested I speak to Madeline. The thought of seeing her made me feel immediately calmer, so I texted her and she said to come and see her as she had a spare appointment. Even though it was difficult to leave the house, I was sure I would feel better for having spoken to her, so I took the Underground to Oxford Circus. Sitting on the Tube, which I'd done a million times before, felt daunting. I felt raw, I couldn't look anyone in the eye for fear of crying and, god forbid, if anyone recognized me, I would have no doubt broken down. I felt like a fragile china doll.

I turned up at a building in central London. The person on the other end of the intercom told me how to open the door. I fiddled with the latch a little but couldn't seem to do it.

There was a man behind me and I could feel him staring, wondering why such a simple task could be taking so long. I tried a few more times until he intervened and opened the door with an eye-roll. I honestly could have burst out crying there and then. It sounds so stupid, but I wanted to say to him, 'Please be patient with me, I can't do stuff any more and I'm really, really frightened.' Of course I was capable of doing stuff, but my brain was telling me that everything was brand-new and I was not to be trusted. I felt as if all the knowledge I'd learnt about being human, sharing spaces, opening doors, taking transport, had regressed to that of a four-year-old. I knew what things were but it was as if I was only just experiencing them on my own for the first time. I was taking a crash course in life and I felt as if I wasn't safe in my own hands.

And while I was learning how to live again, friends and family were moving on with their lives. Grief feels as though the world should stop and everyone should put their lives on hold until we feel better but, of course, looking back, I know this isn't what we really need. The truth is we have to learn how to participate in the world with this new version of ourselves, and it can feel very challenging.

My sister Nicola got engaged not long after Matt's death. Pete, my brother-in-law, had a lovely friendship with Matt. We had started dating around the same time and unbeknown to me Pete and Matt had made an agreement that they would propose some time that year. I found the plans for Matt's proposal on his phone after he died. It was to be in Berlin – and I would have said yes!

When Nicola called me to tell me her news, I was delighted for her. She was elated but I could hear how conflicted she was. She began to cry; she said she felt bad that she and Pete got to carry on their story. I felt the same. So happy that my sister had finally found the man she deserved and yet devastated that Matt was gone. We gave each other understanding and love. Nicola stepped into my shoes for a few minutes and thought about how I might feel. It didn't take away from her happiness, or mine for her. It would have really upset me if she hadn't felt like including me in her happy news. She handled it beautifully.

Grievers know life goes on but I didn't want it to. I wanted it to stop. I wanted to go back to the day before Matt's death and live permanently there. A Groundhog Day that I would be happy to be stuck in in order to avoid the truth.

But there came a point where I felt I needed to accept that the world keeps turning, that it wasn't going to stop for me, and I wanted my friends to understand that, although I had started to accept this, it still felt as if my skin was raw and every new situation was a potential risk of getting hurt.

The anxiety of socializing as a griever is difficult to describe. You want to be included but you don't want to feel obligated. You want to see friends but you need to know you can leave when it gets too much. I felt very, very awkward. It felt as though people were either avoiding me or looking at me with pity. It was all going on in my head.

I had booked a job before Matt died. It was a film about a group of wrestlers trying to save their favourite pub from being shut down. It was called *Walk Like a Panther* and it was a comedy. My character was outrageous in every way. She was called Lara Liplock and she lived for being looked at. She was the antithesis of everything I was feeling and she came to me at the perfect time.

My agent and the director both gave me the opportunity to pull out. They would have understood perfectly, but something inside me felt like it was the right thing to do. So, four months after Matt had died, I did a two-month shoot in Leeds, and for that short period it was as if I was suspended in time. I knew Matt was dead, I wasn't in denial about that. I was completely aware that my work of processing Matt, Dad, and all the other losses in my life was about to begin, and yet for those weeks I gave myself permission to feel good, to laugh as hard as I could and to savour every moment. Because I knew what was waiting for me on the other side, I could enjoy the experience in a way I'd never been able to before.

I was surrounded by the best group of men and women, who laughed and played and worked all day long. We played games every day, silly ones like push penny or who could get the ball into the top of the bottle, games that reminded me of being a kid when you used what you had in front of you. We started putting a quid in for each game to raise the stakes and get even more competitive. It was a fabulous distraction. I felt young again, like I was playing out in my street waiting for my mam to shout me in for my tea. There was a freeness to it. I hadn't felt like that for a long time, even before Matt died. That feeling of being part of a little gang of friends whose only worry was 'What's for tea?' and 'Can I go back out again after?'!

One of the people on set was an older guy who had recently lost his wife. I'd watch him as we waited for a shot to be set up and I could identify with the faraway look in his eyes. The lost look of someone trying to make sense of their new world. I sat next to him one day to ask how he was. I opened up about Matt and his eyes lit up. He knew I knew how he felt. From that day, we both had each other. We made a pact that we didn't have to talk about it all the time but if we gave each other a little look and a nod we were checking in and we would be there if needed.

When you bond over a similar experience the connection can feel intense and very immediate. It's also sometimes fleeting.

For that period of time you have each other and then life goes on. That's what happened on set. We connected but we didn't stay in touch. Back at home, waiting for me were my friends and family. The ones who would be there throughout the ugliness of it all.

How to be a good friend

As a society I think we struggle with going on a journey with our bereaved friends. We tend to do what we think is right at the very start and then peter out fairly quickly. You realize pretty fast who is prepared for the long haul and who would just rather you went back to 'normal'. What I've come to understand over the years is that some of your closest friends may not be the ones who bring you the most comfort, and that's OK. We get upset when people don't meet our needs. When people seem to be getting on with their lives.

I was hyper-vigilant, on high alert at every turn, paranoid that someone may say something or I would see something that would set me off and I would break down. And I was expecting the worst at any second. All of this is why who I spent my time with or who I disclosed to was very important. I had to feel completely safe and trust them 100 per cent.

I was lucky. I had two people in my life that I spoke to daily. One was my sister Nicola. We spoke on the phone every night. The other was Polly. Over the first seven years of our friendship we were to lose two very special men in our lives. Polly's dad, Robin, died of cancer a few years after we met, and in 2023 she lost her aunt Mary, who had been so caring towards me after Matt's death. You never want your friends to be in pain, but Polly's understanding of someone being taken away, of the untimely death of her father, meant that when Matt passed there was no explaining to be done. She got it, and then some. But what was it that she gave me that was so precious? She gave me TULIPS.

> **T**ime – she spent time with me. Sat across a kitchen table. Holding my hand. Sometimes saying nothing but always reminding me she was WITH me.
>
> **U**nderstanding – she never told me my feelings were wrong.
>
> **L**ove – the love was always apparent. Pure acceptance of where I was.
>
> **I**nsight – being able to intuitively understand me through listening and through her own experience. I don't believe that you have to experience grief to be able to be there for a friend like this. If you know what it's like to love then it doesn't take much imagination to imagine what it would be like to lose.
>
> **P**atience – she never got impatient with me. She listened to me talk and never shied away from the intense and uncomfortable feelings.
>
> **S**pace – she always gave me space. To fill it with whatever was coming my way that day. Anger, depression, rage, sadness. She has the gift of not trying to fix, which is one of the most valuable things you can give to a grieving friend.

Not everyone is able to do this. Others gave me other things that were very valuable, but different. Friends would call and chit-chat. They were trying to distract me perhaps, or not upset me? But something I really wanted to say to them in that moment was:

You will NOT upset me by mentioning Matt. You are NOT reminding me. It is ALWAYS at the forefront of my mind. When you don't ask me, it makes me feel isolated and unseen. I want to talk about them and if I cry it's not because you made me; it's because I love them. Taking an interest in our loves makes us feel as if they are closer to us. We want/need them to live on. Not to be banished and never mentioned again.

Many times people would ask about Matt. I would begin to cry as I responded to them. 'Oh no,' they'd say, 'I've upset you.' I would try to explain they hadn't and keep on talking but before I knew it they were on the hunt for a tissue, and in their mission to rescue me – or save themselves from their uncomfortable feelings – they had stopped listening.

If you ask your person about a lost loved one, please wait and listen to the response. YOU didn't make them cry; they are crying because they loved. And don't go searching for a tissue and then hold it in front of their face. All this signals is to please stop crying because you can't bear it and you never really wanted to listen to the answer in the first place.

This is another part of the 'S' of Polly's 'TULIPS'. Space. Grievers need space to grieve. They need people to be able to hold the space without trying to fill or fix it. If you genuinely can't handle someone's grief, please don't ask the question.

Opening up only to be shut down again is worse than never being asked in the first place. It's so lonely and isolating and the message we receive is that we (the whole of us, that is) are not welcome. The griever needs to feel that the whole spectrum of their feelings *are* welcome. Remember, if you ask the question, you may get anger, tears, fear, or any number of reactions. What's important is that you can hold that moment as it is.

I know now that it's important to think carefully about my friends and who I spend time with. If someone makes you feel worse, it's fine, just don't hang out with them. If they ask why, you can always say that you need some time and space to process but will be in touch when you feel ready. If there is a friend who, let's say, isn't such a good listener but is great at taking you out and having fun, then only do that when you're ready and in the mood. It isn't fair on yourself or your friends to spend time with them while simultaneously resenting them.

I learnt this the hard way, though. I felt I had to spend time with people who wanted to spend time with me. People who knew me or Matt and wanted to help. It took me a while to get really comfortable in knowing who I felt good around. I spent an evening having dinner with a few friends not long after Matt died and one of them was lamenting that her family wouldn't be able to have the two holidays they usually have that year and how furious she was that it would only be one. Moments like that told me exactly where I needed to be, and it wasn't there or with her.

It took me even longer to understand that some people have very different ways of dealing with loss and that if their way and yours don't in any way align, that's OK. Set your boundaries and stay true to them. Grief takes up every ounce of energy you have. You do not need to deal with the way others feel about how much you're seeing them. If someone is a true friend then they will wait.

If you're reading this and you are that friend who someone has pulled away from – think. And then think some more. Take your thoughts to a trusted friend who will be honest with you. Be rigorous in your processing and ask yourself these questions:

1. What can I offer my grieving friend?
2. Is what I have to offer valuable to them right now?
3. If my heart was breaking, what would I need from a friend?
4. Can I give them something helpful without needing anything in return?

Placing any sort of demand on a friend who's deep in grief is risky. If you can give them understanding and love then you're halfway there. Whenever I was asked out to an event, I so appreciated the caveat of 'If you're not feeling up to it, then no pressure.'

In the way we put our children first, put your grieving friends before you. Some grievers may be reading this and thinking: 'I don't want to be treated differently, I don't want people to feel sorry for me.' I agree, I didn't either, which is why it's up to the skill and subtlety of the friends around you to do all of this in a way that is protective without making the griever feel pitied. It's tough, I know! It feels like a huge responsibility, but I promise it will pay dividends for the relationship and the griever will never forget the kindness and understanding you showed them.

PART 2
LESSONS IN GRIEF

Chapter 8

How to mend a broken heart

———

My heart felt as though it couldn't do its job any more. I needed to fix something, but I didn't know how or have the energy. What I did know, instinctively, was that the way I put it back together would be the most important part.

The film shoot ended and I came home. I had been staying in Leeds, and being in a different city and living space had helped me separate myself from my reality. I had pressed the pause button but I knew I had to go back. And, when I did return, I fell into a deep slump. I was bereft.

It didn't surprise me; I had been expecting it. I wasn't running away but I was certainly delaying. I wouldn't have been able to play someone quite as forthright as Lara Liplock if I hadn't put my pain to one side for a moment. The important part here is that I did return to my grief. I had to. I had made a promise to myself and I wasn't going to break it. I'd also been taught a valuable lesson. I had experienced joy on that set. Fleeting, yes, but it let me know that I was still capable of feeling that way. I now believed that joy was going to be a part of my life again. I remembered who I was and that I had something to offer.

Despite me knowing all of this AND believing it, grieving isn't linear, and my body returned to the heavy burden of grief.

I ached; my bones and feet hurt. I didn't have energy and I felt at least twenty years older – but more than that my heart hurt, really hurt. It was physically painful. Sometimes my heart heaved out of my chest, sometimes it felt tight, and other times it felt as though it was falling through my body. Tiny little fragments making their way down. Atrophy, always atrophy. Never in my life had I understood the phrase 'a fragile heart' more.

I have loved, I have lost, and my heart is indeed broken. I *felt* it; it was heavy and restrictive. The tightness made me feel as though I couldn't breathe. The feeling of space and expansion I had felt on set had left me, and now I was contracting again. I knew it would pass and yet somehow every time I was in a contraction I found it hard to believe I would ever return. This only exacerbated the feelings. Sometimes the contractions would be on me as I woke up. I would feel OK the night before but wake with the dread and constriction. Other times it would be a slow demise. A feeling of agonizing sadness that happened over a few days. Trying to alleviate the panic of feeling myself tighten, I always told myself that everything was allowed, it was ALL welcome. I tried to accept it all as part of the process, and even though I hated every moment, I would try my best to see what I could learn from it.

My heart felt as though it couldn't do its job any more. I needed to fix something, but didn't know how or have the energy. What I did know, instinctively, was that the way I put it back together would be the most important part.

The tools I acquired and the lessons I learnt on the road to healing have now become the building blocks for my life. I have taken wisdom from friends, family, grievers, books, 12-step programmes and grief retreats. Once you begin to look there is an abundance of help and knowledge out there for all of us who find ourselves grieving and can't see a way out. For the next part of this book I would like to take you with me on my journey of discovery and show you what I've learnt. The things that helped me feel as though my grief doesn't have to overshadow me or define me. I want to give you the tools that have been handed to me so that you can use whatever is useful to you. Our grief lives with us, but it doesn't always have to be an unwelcome visitor. I would also love you to keep in mind that all these lessons can be useful to help others too. You may not be grieving right now but someone you love may benefit from your understanding of it. I'd also ask you to hold this thought, something I learnt that changed my attitude to grieving: loss is not just bereavement. What we grieve isn't always tangible. You may be grieving the end of a relationship, a loss of hope, career, innocence or any number of disappointments and course changes in your life. We have hopes and dreams for ourselves that don't always come to fruition. We tend to either dismiss or wallow in them, but if you find the pain keeps returning and is holding you back then there is most likely some grief work to be done. Hopefully the lessons I've learnt will also help you navigate your way through grief and clear the path that may be blocking your progress.

Looking back to my twenties, I can see that I was looking for something or someone to fix me. I needed to feel whole, so I looked to people, places and things to fulfil the parts of me that I couldn't reach myself. I hadn't learnt yet that the journey had to begin internally before any of the external could make any sense. Once I began my sober journey, this became very clear to me. I realized the importance of healthy boundaries. I had veered between shutting down and refusing to allow others in and allowing people to treat me in ways I didn't deserve. After Matt's death, something happened that put me in danger of shutting down completely. For Christmas 2016, he had given me a gold necklace. It looked like a piece of treasure found at the bottom of the ocean. It was an imperfect round shape and it had tiny blue sapphires in it. I adored it and I knew I would for ever. After his death, it became even more precious, not only because it was a beautiful gift but because I knew he had touched it and it made me feel connected to him. Six months later and after much deliberation, I decided to buy myself a ring. It was a beautiful turquoise stone with rubies either side. I had coveted this ring for quite some time and Polly and I always joked that once we felt a proposal was imminent she would guide Matt to this ring and let him know that was *the* one. In the aftermath of losing him and deep in grief, Polly encouraged me to buy myself the ring. It would be a symbol of our love and a symbol to me that I could also love myself. I treasured it, and even though I'm not hugely sentimental with 'things', I have always loved and looked after my jewellery.

Just over a year after Matt died, I was back up north celebrating my mam's seventieth birthday. We had hired a house for her, and the whole family came. We ate, we talked and we played games. I was enjoying being around everyone but I was feeling very raw after Matt's first anniversary. We were just about to start a board game when I got a message from my lovely neighbour Rachel. My front window was smashed and she could see I wasn't at home. It transpired that I had been burgled. There were lots of things that could have been taken from the flat, but the only thing they were interested in was my jewellery. The necklace and ring were gone and, in that moment, I could almost feel the walls building up around my heart. The sound of my family's well-meaning comments – 'You can buy another one'; 'Make sure you claim on the insurance' – all felt futile. I went to my room and lay on the bed. The feeling of loss overwhelmed me. To lose Dad and Matt was unbearable, yet someone taking my jewellery – something that meant nothing apart from money to them – was cruel. I felt as though the world didn't want to give me a break. I felt angry and as though it would be best to block everyone and everything out. It wasn't worth it. The sense of things being taken and taken and taken, when all the while I was just trying to get on, completely broke me in that moment. The world didn't feel safe enough to be in any more.

A broken heart

Now I know that our hearts break all the time and they are clever enough to repair themselves. But if we don't take the time to put them back together with our complete care and attention, then we may find that we are constantly struggling. I was in danger of closing down after that experience, but thankfully I had learnt that over time that would have been even more painful and would have blocked my road to healing.

I'd like you to visualize your emotional self as a physical heart. In a neutral position, it still has space and holes for feelings to flow in and out. A healthy heart can receive and give love. It has boundaries and it takes care of who and what it allows in. It is receptive and discerning. But when our hearts break, they feel like they are smashed into a million little pieces. Mine certainly did. I felt as though my heart was falling through my body, trying to find its way back home.

What we have to do is put it back together. This will take time, probably longer than you think, and you must treat yourself as you would a newborn baby: with gentle care and lots of attention. If we don't, one of these two scenarios may happen.

A closed heart

When our hearts break, we feel the need to put them back together quickly and with force because we are scared. We focus so much on the repair that we don't take time to understand the breakages in the first place. Our only focus is to get back to 'normal'. To carry on and to 'be strong'. The problem we encounter here, is if you try to speed up a healing process, there will be a price to pay.

When we fall and hurt ourselves, the scab heals on its own timescale. When our bones break, they can only fuse back together in the time our body allows. We have to honour the process. We wear the cast and we wait until our body informs us it's time to walk again. We don't do this with our heart. We don't give our heartbreak the same respect. We get frightened because there isn't a timeline. No one can tell us when we will feel better, so we take matters into our own hands and we run as fast as we can towards a feeling of normality. Trying to reach for something vaguely like the person we were before.

But we're not the same person any more and it takes time to get know this new being, with all their unfamiliar thoughts and emotions. 'Fixing' the heart so quickly can result in real difficulties with relationships in the future. Let me explain it like this.

If you rush to repair without much reflection, then you will build a fortress that no one will be able to break through. You will have used far too many bricks and way too much cement because you had no idea what you were trying to cover. You threw everything you had at it and didn't stop until the walls were high and thick enough. Then, when you finally take a breath and decide you're ready to go back into the world, you will find that it's difficult for you to let people in.

The closed heart we are left with has a wall so high and impenetrable that it's no longer capable of vulnerability and real intimacy. It believes these are things to be avoided because they could bring the walls crashing down and cause the heart to shatter into a million pieces again. People, hopes and dreams are to be avoided because they can disappoint and cause heartbreak. The closed heart doesn't lose anything (or so it thinks) because it never lets anything in. It stays walking on the same road, going in the same direction, because it feels safe.

Only, this is an illusion, and it can only protect you for a short time. You will struggle with real intimacy because the fear of another heartbreak is so present. The pain is still there inside those walls. All you have done is build a barrier around it. You will defend it until your last breath and I get it, I really do – it feels terrifying to be open to pain again. But these defences are exhausting and will leave us feeling lonely. We will be desperate for connection but we will struggle to find it, because we are not really connected to ourselves.

In order to heal, we have to understand the pain. It's not enough to tell ourselves 'we've lost a loved one'. We have to get detailed, specific.

When Matt died I had to admit how much I felt as if I was being punished and abandoned. I had to admit that I believed that I must be a bad person. The temptation here was to build that wall, to never let anyone back in because the pain wasn't worth it. The feeling of being cursed meant I could have easily locked myself in my very own tower and protected myself from all the 'badness'. Thankfully, because of my therapy and all the wisdom I had picked up from the rooms of AA, I instinctively felt this wouldn't be the best thing to do, but believe me when I say I was certainly tempted.

The over-expanded heart

When we keep the heart completely expanded all the time, we allow anything or anyone in, without boundaries or discernment. We are so desperate to be 'fixed' that we give people permission to enter our lives so *they* can fix us.

The heart stays wide open and people are allowed to come and go as they please. We feel walked over, abandoned, taken advantage of. We are so exposed and fragile and devoid of boundaries that other people become our gatekeepers, which leads to insecurity, low self-esteem and, eventually, resentment. The irony is that both closed heart and over-expanded heart are looking for the same thing. Both want to find a way back to a love and connection that feels safe and secure. Unfortunately, neither way helps us because they've both taken short cuts.

The overly expanded heart has left itself wide open in the hope it will be fixed by outside influences. It believes its openness will make it more lovable and it will be put back together by someone or something wiser and stronger. It places itself into the hands of otherness and then shouts and screams when that doesn't live up to expectations. When the new job isn't fulfilling enough, the new relationship stops fixing us, the new house and the new town we've moved to stop feeling exciting and we are back with the emptiness and tight feelings in our chest. This is the empty bucket, and this was me for so long. Always hoping that the next 'thing' would be the one to make me feel as though I'd arrived. To destination happiness! Or, more presciently in my case, destination contentment.

The over-expanded heart wants to let anyone and anything in so it doesn't have to face things alone.

The closed heart lives life at half mast, never allowing real joy and vulnerability in for fear of it breaking.

Both are lives half lived. Neither way is going to get us to where we deserve to be.

What we want is a healthy, boundaried heart. A heart that discerns.

To live a life full of love and tenderness and commitment we need to be able to take accountability for ourselves AND we need to protect and love ourselves. Our hearts need to be put back together with care and precision. People can and will help but ultimately we are responsible for our own progress.

The unreliable partner is exciting for a while. The big new house is a symbol of success until we can't pay the mortgage. The drink makes us feel happy until it doesn't. We cannot fix our insides from the outside. I have tried all of these things and every time I've become angry and resentful that it hasn't worked. I have been annoyed with partners for not fulfilling me, resentful at my overblown mortgage payments and my stupidity for getting myself there in the first place, and furious at alcohol for not working the way I want it to any more. What I needed to do was to put my heart back together carefully and with patience. To attend to its pieces and process all the feelings that had broken it in the first place.

Making friends with our grief

Grieving is loving. It's an outpouring of devotion for the person that has gone. Grief has an energy and a force that is unpredictable but the way we respond and interact with that force can allow us to feel as though it's not just happening *to* us, but rather we are in a process, an unfolding of sorts. Our response may not always be tears. It may be anger, frustration, anxiety, depression. It can wear many different hats, but ultimately the process only asks for your time and attention. The heart needs to allow those feelings to flow. It needs to understand what it has lost so it can come back together and feel whole again. It will feel different. But different isn't always bad . . .

When we are in pain, we long to get back to a feeling of normality, to feel ourselves again. We need to feel how we used to, to break free of the unfamiliar emotions in our bodies. We feel like strangers to ourselves. The way we think and feel has changed so profoundly that it scares us. Living without the person we have lost is painful enough, but feeling like the world we live in is unrecognizable is too much to bear. So off we go, to anything that feels or sounds like home, something that soothes us because it's what we know.

At first it feels great, like we might be able to survive. It seems surmountable. We see friends, fill up our diaries, go back to work and continue with our lives. The normality calms us and our brain begins to think that we might just be OK. What we're not prepared for is the unravelling.

Rushing our grieving process and not putting ourselves back together gently is a bit like looking something up on Google. Before we've barely asked ourselves the question the phone is out and we've retrieved the answer. There was no thought, no patience to see if we could get there in our minds. No stretching of ourselves to try to reach the answer. The hard work has been done for us. The relief is immediate and momentary. The chances of retaining the answer are pretty low because we didn't do the work to get there. And so it is in grief.

If we rush, if we hurtle towards feeling good again, then the relief will be temporary and the realization of this will be even more painful than if we had been patient with ourselves in the first place. The number of times I've been angry with myself and screamed, 'I thought I was past this, I thought this had been dealt with!' What I really mean is: 'I don't want to visit this place again, I don't want to have to go back to this dark and frightening place again.'

But go back we must. Again and again and again and each time there will be a new lesson, each time we will lighten the load of grief, but only if we listen. The way to mend our hearts is to make friends with our grief. Not to push it away but to invite it in, like an old friend. It's not our enemy; it wants to help, but it can only do so if we work with it and not against it.

Sometimes I talk to my grief. Firstly, I acknowledge it's there. The truth is it's always there but there are times when it feels particularly overbearing. The gut reaction is to push it away and when I do, it always makes it worse. I feel completely disconnected from myself. I griefwalk through my day; I'm there but I'm not present. Either I'm shut down and can't be honest with people or I'm on the brink of tears, which means I appear abrupt and harsh – God forbid anyone asking me how I am!

So, in those moments of overwhelm, I take a breath and invite the grief in. I ask it to sit alongside me, agree that I will listen to it and observe it and not push it away. I ask it to be gentle with me. I might ask it to be aware that I have a lot of work on today so it needs to be mindful that I have to function highly, or I might suggest that this is a day when I can turn myself over to it fully. The most important thing here is connecting with it. The grief is part of me, after all, it's who I am. I allow compassion for that part of myself as I would a friend.

It's amazing what happens when I do this. It's magical. It

allows me to be able to function and go through my day without feeling that I am either a robot or a tsunami waiting to happen.

But in order to keep my heart healthy and allow it to come back together in a way that will serve me, I have to try to accept what it brings me each and every day.

Chapter 9

My grief reveals itself

———

Looking back, I can see that grief was showing itself to me in lots of different ways. It tried on many different costumes and I definitely didn't always recognize it.

I think many of us believe that if we are ignoring our grief we can escape it. Many of us override our internal software for so long and so vehemently that we can actually trick ourselves into thinking it's gone away. How many times have you heard someone refer to a traumatic event in their lives and say, 'I just don't feel anything any more. It really doesn't affect me.' I believe that something a little closer to the truth would be that they have moved so far away from the pain, repeatedly disconnecting with it, that when they do recall the event the body and the brain simply don't react any more. They have literally trained themselves to not feel. Or at least not feel in a way that is too painful. But the body and the brain are way cleverer than that. While we believe the hurt has gone away, it has simply been de-prioritized. We have filed it away to be looked at when the time feels right.

But that time never comes, because the longer we ignore it the more the grief begins to metastasize as the pain takes on a different shape and we no longer recognize it. Which is why when people say that it doesn't bother them any more or that they just don't feel anything it's because the feelings attached to the loss have been severed. It makes way for something else. Something often unrecognizable to us. But the body keeps the score. It stores anything we are not processing and it doesn't matter how hard we distract ourselves or how many 'mountains we climb', the relief won't last unless we do all of the work.

It's hard to hear that grief is work, but the gifts that await you on the other side of the pain are truly transformative.

Looking back, I can see that grief was showing itself to me in lots of different ways. It tried on many different costumes and I definitely didn't always recognize it. I want to show you some of the disguises it wears for me and the sneaky ways it still catches me out. I realize it will show up differently for all of us, but you may just connect or identify with some of the examples and find it helpful moving forward.

Leaky anger

My son attended an out-of-school maths learning programme and, a month or so after Matt died, I called them to say he wouldn't be returning. I explained our personal situation and they seemed sympathetic. I thanked them and thought nothing more of it. The next day they called to tell me that I was a day too late cancelling and that I would have to pay for the next month. They explained they were a small, family-led company and this was their policy.

What I should have done is politely remind them under what circumstances I was leaving and ask them to seriously reconsider. What I did instead was ask how they could possibly call themselves a family company and not take my situation into consideration. How despicable it was not to show compassion towards me and make me pay another month for a service I could no longer attend.

My point was valid, but after I put the phone down I was upset at the way I handled myself. The emotive language I used and the fact that I got so upset on the phone didn't seem to match the situation. I was in total overwhelm. I just needed to breathe, to respond and not react, but I couldn't. That's why it's called *leaky* anger. Anger is often a secondary emotion, a sign of something else that is not being given attention, such as sadness, disappointment or fear.

Have you ever found yourself becoming irrationally angry or reactive with a bus driver who didn't wait for you, or a shop assistant who can't give you what you need?

What about being held on the end of the telephone line only to be told that you're through to the wrong department?

Now before you scream at me, 'But, Jill, these *are* really irritating situations. Anyone would get angry,' I know! Believe me, I do not need convincing. I was always an impatient child. It would be the criticism levelled at me the most often and still something to this day my son has to challenge me on.

My energy is pretty fast and I often run on adrenaline. The traumas I have experienced particularly with sudden death mean I struggle with hyper-vigilance. Harvey is far more level and will often remind me to slow down a little when he sees me getting impatient in a queue or if I feel someone isn't being efficient enough. It's pretty embarrassing to write this down but I do need reminding. The very old feelings of unmet needs from when I was a little girl can still reveal themselves when I feel things aren't quite going right or that I've lost control.

When we hold our grief it stays stuck inside of us. We

think we are doing a great job of holding it down, but what we don't realize is that suppressing it is actually taking a huge amount of energy from us. Among loved ones there is someone to hold us accountable if we react out of proportion, but in the anonymous spaces of bus stations and supermarkets we lose some awareness, the valve bursts and we find ourselves overreacting.

When you look back at one of these reactions that you may have had, you may think to yourself, *Wow, that was really over the top, I totally lost my temper for what now seems pretty insignificant!* I've found myself in these scenarios so many times and what I now know is that there is more work to be done. There is a saying that goes: 'If it's hysterical, it's historical.' This is a really simple phrase to help guide me where I need to go next.

Personally, I need to go back to some of those old feelings of abandonment and despair and tell myself that this is not what is happening now. The feeling of panic and not being in control may feel the same in my body but my brain can separate these events very easily if I talk to it rationally. I can tell myself that this may feel familiar but it is not the same, and then I ask myself this question . . .

Are you breathing?

I know it sounds stupid, right. But more often than not I'm shallow breathing, which is breathing purely from the top of my chest and the breaths are short and sharp.

Eckhart Tolle, the German spiritual teacher, writes so clearly about this in his seminal book *The Power of Now*. He explains that if we can find the awareness in these situations to just breathe we can often avoid the overwhelming reaction.

He asks us to take three deep breaths mindfully. This means really concentrating on the breath entering and exiting our bodies. Allow yourself to really feel the oxygen entering your lungs. Concentrate on this for three full breaths.

Almost immediately things will become clearer. This sounds ridiculously simple. It's not a fixer. It's a pause button.

I wasn't able to have that foresight in my conversation with the maths company. It was too late – I had reacted before I became aware. And this is OK: we may *only* become aware once we have reacted and said something we regret, but what the breath gives us is the perspective to slow down, apologize and gain some insight.

This is going to happen to all of us at some point, but if we are experiencing leaky anger on a fairly regular basis then it's definitely time to ask some more questions.

Have I spoken today to someone I trust about how I feel?

Say it, don't store it. Once we are honest about our feelings and we have been listened to, it's incredible how much easier it is to be with our feelings. Sometimes all I need to do is be really honest with someone.

Have I done anything today that I KNOW makes me feel better?

E.g., exercise, walking, listening to music, connecting with nature, meditating. If not, do at least one. A quick walk around the block can help me if I only have five minutes to spare. Anything to get out of my head and into my body. Playing a song really loudly and singing at the top of my lungs helps too. Singing as if nobody is listening is impossible to do without it releasing something inside us. It's a way I can get out of my thoughts and into my feelings. Meditating and slowing right down is often all I need. My tendency to run on adrenaline means I often experience burnout, but if I'm on top of all the above it keeps me grounded and steadied.

It's so easy for me to ask myself this question and think, *No, I haven't done any of those things but that's because I've had a million other things to do first!*

Looking after ourselves takes real discipline and this question is imperative to give yourself the best chance of healing. Whenever I allow these actions to slip for a number of days I find the negative effects start to build up very quickly.

Endings

Unprocessed grief has often shown up for me as a real difficulty with 'endings'. My experience as a kid of struggling with the ending of the production of *Annie*, my anxiety around our family gatherings coming to an end or basically anything that filled me up and distracted me. Finding it really difficult to process the ending of something we've enjoyed is understandable but for us grievers it's more than that. It's because we know what awaits us. A deep emptiness, a void that needs to be filled with the next 'thing'.

The sadness that was lurking beneath the surface had a chance to take centre stage in these moments. The grief had been on standby since Dad died and was waiting to engulf me once it could sense I was vulnerable and I had slowed down.

This feeling didn't just reveal itself in big moments either. I would struggle when we had family over for tea. There would be a sense of togetherness in the house. There was laughter and connection – and the minute I heard the first auntie announce they were leaving I knew it wouldn't be long before everyone followed suit. I would feel an inappropriate amount of disappointment.

Of course I didn't understand any of this; all I knew at the time was that I would wake up the next day feeling bereft, as if something had been ripped from me, stolen, and I would never see it again.

Even then, as a child, I would be thinking, *Jeez, Jill, they'll be back. Calm down.* But that was my little warrior talking to me. The part of me that told me to pull myself together. That nothing bad was really happening. The part of me that had stopped looking at or listening to what was underneath. I was taking things at face value because that's what I had unknowingly trained myself to do.

This is what happens when grief is unattended to. It finds places to live, to lurk, it bends itself into shapes that seem unrecognizable, but with a little investigation we see what it really is. It takes a bit of courage and patience to keep asking yourself what it is that's underneath your reaction. Let's take my example of the family leaving the house when I was little; the kind of questions you could ask yourself are below. It's really important to answer them as honestly as possible, and to try not to approach them from an adult, rational state of mind, because the gold we are digging for is often buried in the emotional child part of us.

Am I sad they are leaving? . . . Yes.

Why? . . . Because I've had a great time and I like them.

How does the noise make you feel? . . . Happy, full, distracted.

How do you feel when they leave? . . . Sad, empty, inside my own head again.

How does the house feel when they're gone? . . . Quiet, depressing, lonely.

Why? . . . Because it feels like something is missing.

When did you last feel as if something was missing? . . . When Dad died.

Do you think your family will come back? . . . I hope so but I can't be sure.

Do you think you are able to feel happy and full without lots of people around you? . . . I don't know how to do that yet.

So already from those few questions you can see where my work is needed. I'm an adult now and I have learnt that I can be alone and feel happy and fulfilled, but it took investigation and work and patience to get there. I learnt some of this from my 12-step programme, where we are invited to interrogate our thoughts. Not to punish myself but to make sure that I have an understanding of where the pain is coming from. Once I can locate it, I can move towards healing it.

Asking yourself these questions is a really simple exercise, but it's deceptively powerful.

Sometimes we really are angry or sad at what is exactly in

front of us. But to investigate, all it takes is a moment, a breath, a pause, and to ask ourselves one question. Is this really what I'm sad about? We have to stay close to ourselves, and if, like me, you weren't taught how, it's never too late. Never. My struggle with endings, for example, was a really clear way through the investigation for me. It was obvious that the feeling didn't match the situation. Other situations aren't quite so obvious, so even if something feels just a little bit off, still ask the questions. Keep communicating with yourself. The relationship we have with ourselves is by far the most important relationship we will ever have. It informs the quality of all the other relationships we have in our lives. Never stop talking to yourself, build a relationship that is precious to you, as precious as all the other relationships you have; always check in with how you're doing – and make sure to listen!

Criticism

I remember feeling really embarrassed when my son expressed his opinion about his packed lunch to me one day. He was trying to explain that he hadn't been enjoying it and was asking for what he would actually prefer to eat. I was a bit snippy and irritable with him. Surely any good mam in the world would just KNOW what their son wanted. He was being so mature and clear and yet all I heard was: 'You can't get anything right, can you?'

I was offended, over a packed lunch!!!

The inability to handle criticism may seem a million miles away from grief, but it's actually inextricably linked. The more

139

we store the sadness and pain, the less capacity we have for anything that may be challenging or uncomfortable.

Just check in with yourself and be honest. Do you find it difficult to receive criticism even if it's constructive? Do you find being challenged a feeling that's so uncomfortable that your reaction to it is childish and ineffective?

The criticism can come from anywhere at any time, as with the moment around Harvey's packed lunch. What I was actually feeling was a sense of not being able to cope with the seemingly most basic of tasks. That not only was I a grieving mam, but my son had the worst packed lunch in school so I was failing at that too! Seems ridiculous to think of it now but we have to acknowledge that walking through grief is challenging and it doesn't do us any favours to have others believe we have it all under control. We don't.

This tucking away of our pain, storing it neatly in our deep dark cupboards, can mean it escapes and turns up where we least expect. We like to imagine it's ordered, in its proper place, and if we did want to find it we would know exactly where it was.

But the truth is that unprocessed grief is messy. It's stuffed into those cupboards and they're bursting at the seams! But as long as nobody sees inside we can pretend, right? As long as no one opens the door then we are in control of what everyone else gets to see. The perfection image. Those of us who want everyone to know we are doing just fine. Not because we are, but because we feel if someone tugs at the threads just a little we will unravel and may never stop. Keeping up this image is exhausting and it means when anyone dares to question or challenge us, it feels as though the house of cards will come tumbling down.

If we were a little more honest with those around us, our friends, employers etc., we wouldn't feel so attacked when we are questioned. If we were more capable of being honest and letting, let's say, our boss know that today is a particularly bad day and we are struggling, then we wouldn't be so afraid when our work is discussed.

If we drop the mask of perfection and let people in a little then we would be able to agree or receive criticism with perspective. We might even be able to say, 'Yes, I agree. My work hasn't been great today but I did try my best. My grief is overwhelming me right now but I am aware.'

What we need to avoid is control. Allowing is what we are aiming for, but allowing grief is sometimes terrifying to me, because it feels out of control. There are certain areas of my life where I have exerted a huge amount of control. And it may not always seem obvious to look at.

I went through a phase of being really frustrated with my son when he lost things at school. Anything from a water bottle to a coat or a scooter. It didn't matter how big or small, my frustration and need to find them would always be the same. I would say to him 'You have to look after your things, it's important that you remember what you have and bring them home.' I would criticize him for being forgetful and not caring about his possessions. What I see now is a little boy who no doubt had a huge amount on his mind and felt distracted a lot;

I also see a woman who felt so out of control on the inside that she was holding on very tight for order and structure on the outside. The criticism levelled at Harvey was really me being unable to accept the uncomfortable truth of feeling untethered.

Difficulty leaning on others

When I was a little girl I used to love the days when I was allowed to walk home from school on my own. Not because I enjoyed the solitude but because it eradicated the anxiety I would feel about my mam turning up for me. By the way, my mam always turned up, but it didn't stop the feeling that one day she might not, so it was easier to remove that worry from my day. The feeling of disappointment of being let down somehow gets lumped in with abandonment, and if I'm not careful it can all feel the same.

I find it hard to accept and feel comfortable with offered help. It's not that I don't want it, it's that I find it harder being let down than doing the job myself. It's easier for me to struggle through a task than to worry someone may not turn up or make me feel beholden to them. I worry it won't be done right or how I would do it. I can't stand the thought of someone being helpful and me not being able to be grateful because I'm not happy with the outcome. It's all mixed up with my unmet needs as a child and a belief that things won't work out so I need to be in control. Maybe this chimes with you too?

The truth is I often feel way more comfortable *not* getting what I want. It feels pretty safe there. I battle with this part of myself but I try to practise compassion. I understand that it goes way back to Dad dying. I was abandoned by a primary caregiver at a time when I needed them so desperately. My internal programming told me that I had to look after myself, that no one was coming to save me. The heartbroken part of me wasn't able to tell itself that one person leaving doesn't mean everyone will.

If we don't process properly we tend to think in big, un-nuanced ideas because the belief is based on a feeling rather than fact.

The fact is my father died suddenly and I felt abandoned.

The belief is anyone I put my faith or trust in will leave me.

This is a giant leap and deeply unhelpful to me, which is why processing it is fundamental to my healing.

Let me take a moment here to talk about some of the things I've learnt about core beliefs and some examples of how they may show up.

Some of you may have lost a loved one to a very slow and painful illness. As a result, you may now have a deep-rooted belief that it would be inappropriate for you to feel happy or to thrive because you have watched your loved one die in such pain. As a result you stop looking after yourself and stop giving your body what it needs to be healthy and happy.

A romantic partner who left you heartbroken may result in you disallowing yourself from falling in love again. If you haven't been able to recognize the grief and how it has manifested, it may result in you being too frightened to love again because love means pain to you.

The loss of a dream job or promotion may stop you from ever pushing yourself to go for something you really want in the future. The pain of rejection may seem too unbearable to experience again, if you haven't allowed the grief of the original disappointment to express itself properly. I found it useful to think about the loss of Dad and Matt and then make a list of what the facts were surrounding that and what my beliefs were. Of course we all already have core beliefs about who we are, based on our upbringing, influences and genetics. But what happens in grief is that we are so vulnerable and exhausted that we don't challenge the beliefs. We accept them because we *feel* them so deeply. By the time we have more strength and perspective they have been ingrained in us as a fact, a truth, an absolute. Whenever I would feel myself having these same continuous and demoralizing thoughts, I had to take a beat and ask myself these questions:

1. Is this true?
2. Can you absolutely know it's true?
3. How do you react/what happens when you believe the thought?
4. Who would you be without that thought?

So let's take one of my core beliefs as an example.

Belief: *Everyone I love will eventually leave/abandon me.*

1. Is this true?

No. Two very significant and important people have left me but many people who I love dearly are still in my life.

2. Can you absolutely know it's true?

No. I know rationally that it isn't true. But sometimes it feels that way. So I can attach a feeling of disappointment or being let down to this core belief. It isn't true factually, but my body can make me believe it.

3. How do you react/what happens when you believe the thought?

I feel scared and hopeless. I feel as though the safest way to live is to rely on no one and expect nothing. It makes me feel as though opening my heart to anyone new is going to kill me because I don't believe I can take another heartbreak.

4. Who would you be without that thought?

A more open and joyful person. Someone with boundaries but who can love with abandon. Someone who can accept that people come and go and it is no reflection on how lovable I am.

These questions are from *The Work* by the wonderful Katie Byron and, although they are not specific to grief, I have found them very useful in my approach to loss.

Often we just need to unlock a different way of thinking to

understand what exactly we want and just how much we are getting in our own way.

Depression

Dear Matt, I argued with my mam tonight. It's so uncomfortable to have to spell out how much pain you're in. She said, 'Are you feeling a little bit low today?' I screamed, 'NO! I'm feeling utterly devastated!' She knows, she understands, she gets it, but we're not used to talking to each other like that, Matt. The world functions on platitudes and niceties. I want to scream, shout, punch and kick. I was out for a walk with Harvey yesterday and we were playing with sticks. I was trying to break mine in two, whacking it really hard against a tree. I could feel all my rage and energy going into breaking this stick. My god it felt good!

Grief felt like a strange weight inside me. A heavy entity that threatened access to all my other feelings. There were times when I felt I needed to break through this energy force so that I could connect with what was underneath it. If I didn't, it left me feeling numb and depressed, which for me was a lot scarier. Trying to break the stick against the tree and my annoyance with my mam on the phone is my attempt to access those feelings and not hide them under a general feeling of depression. The feeling of being weighed down sent me into a panic for fear of not having the strength to fight back one day. 'Depress' comes from the Latin verb *deprimere*, to press down, which feels like a perfect definition as that's exactly how it feels. However, I've come to feel like the word 'depressed' is used so often now that the true meaning has been lost, and perhaps we say it to avoid being specific and honest with ourselves and others.

As the months rolled by and other people asked how I was, I wasn't brave or comfortable enough to reply to them as I had with Mam. 'Distraught', 'angry', 'inconsolable' were the words that would spring to mind. But before I could muster the energy, they would say, 'You must be depressed.'

'Yeah, yeah, I guess I am,' I would reply quietly. Somehow I felt *they* were more comfortable with that word. It was more palatable to them. It felt dismissive, but I didn't have the confidence to explain myself, so I'd agree. And, to be fair, in that moment they were right, absolutely on point. I was indeed pressing down. Squashing anything that seemed too real or too hard to digest. I felt worse, I felt heavier and more isolated.

It seems obvious to say depression would be an outcome of grief but what I wanted to touch upon here is that the word depressed seems to have become a huge umbrella under which we describe our feelings. I'm not talking about clinical depression or any condition that is being treated medically. I'm talking about the way we use it in our everyday language to avoid saying how we really feel.

Think about it like this: you're at the water cooler on Monday morning feeling wretched. Your colleague/friend asks how your weekend has been and you say, 'Oh, it was fine. Didn't get up to much and feeling pretty depressed. Can't believe it's Monday again to be honest.'

Your friend doesn't bat an eyelid and either says, 'Yeah, same,' or, 'Oh well, it will be Friday before you know it.'

The word depressed has become a blanket term that we use to explain anything from insecurities about our bodies, being skint or bored, to the other extreme of our deep, deep grief. We don't flinch when someone uses it because we feel comfortable with its ubiquity. But imagine a conversation back at the water cooler that may be more honest and specific about our feelings.

'How was your weekend?'

'It was difficult. I really struggle at the weekends because the loneliness feels overwhelming. I try to do things to take my mind off it but I just feel really sad.'

When you read that sentence did you think, *OMG, I would never say that. Not in a million years, feels way too vulnerable?* I'm gonna guess that most of us would have had that reaction, but aren't we saying the same thing in the first example, just with different words?

Depression will find a way to stay in our body and weigh us down. After time we get used to the weight and it begins to feel like it's part of us. Like a very heavy coat. We go through life and forget it's even there but after years of wearing it we begin to tire, everything feels difficult until eventually even our spirit feels weighed down. This is what it feels like to store pain; heavy, relentless and depressing.

So what I'm challenging you to do here is the next time you say you feel depressed, ask yourself: 'Why? What do I feel depressed about?'

If you reply, 'I've lost someone I love! Of course I'm depressed!', then ask the next question.

'How does it make you feel to be without them?'

My thoughts usually go something like this:

I miss them.

It makes me feel really sad to not be able to hear their voice.

I want to share things with them and see them smile.

The longer they have been gone the further away I feel from them and myself.

When something good happens and I can't tell them I feel like the world will never feel as fun as it did when they were here.

Try to stay with the questions and to dwell in the detail. This will help inform us of what we need to do next.

It's a relief to know why you feel a certain way. Too often we generalize and say, 'It's just everything,' but it's not everything, not if we are prepared to break it down.

You know when you go to the doctor with a problem and they explain why you have been feeling the way you have and you immediately feel relief? It's like that.

You may be reading this and thinking, 'Jill, why would knowing exactly why I feel so terrible be better than just feeling terrible?' Because it helps us understand! Which in turn helps release the pain and, most importantly, allows ourselves compassion.

If we can be honest and specific about our feelings to ourselves and to our trusted loved ones we will begin to feel less alone.

If we truly understand something we have a much higher chance of being able to cope with it. We then have a choice to do something about it, something that may lead us to greater understanding and healing.

I suggest that you reject the general feeling of depression you have in your body and keep asking yourself, 'What exactly is this feeling?' 'What specifically am I missing today?' Don't be afraid; it's a relief. It won't make you feel worse; it will make you feel more compassion for yourself.

There may be times, however, when our thoughts and our questions make us feel even more confused. The more we ask, the more annoyed we get at not knowing the answer. Then the frustration kicks in and before we know it we are berating ourselves. This is when using mantras becomes really helpful. I suppose my first experience of using a mantra was my 'I don't want to dream' as I drifted off to a wishful dreamless sleep as a child. But my 12-step programme taught me that I could use them in many different scenarios. Once, talking to a friend, I told them I found my incessant overthinking very unhelpful on the days where I needed clarity and nothing but more questions were coming back to me. He looked at me and said, 'Oh yeah, I know that feeling. On those days I just ask to get out of my own way. I use the mantra "Please remove me from the obsession of my own thoughts." It really helps me.'

It was like a light bulb. A small mantra that could get me out of the way of me and help calm my head down. So on my worst days grieving, feeling as though I'm being dragged through a storm, helpless and out of control, with too many questions and too few answers, these little mantras help me to centre myself and focus. If you want to give them a try, it's best not to focus on something you *don't* want. For example: 'Please don't let anything bad happen to (insert name) today.'

This feels like an anxious prayer. Asking for something or someone to intervene to save us. I feel they work best when they are autonomous and empowering. And, if you find it hard to do at first, just stay with it. I often find myself repeating these on the toilet as it's a place I know I won't be disturbed!

The most important thing about your chosen mantra is to ask with complete willingness and sincerity. Then get quiet enough to listen, and you will hear yourself and the answers. Here is another one I use that you may find helpful: 'Please open my heart and let me hear myself clearly. Please open my heart and let me hear myself clearly. Please open my heart and let me hear myself clearly.'

Inability to access joy

There were many days after losing Matt where I was having a perfectly nice time with friends or family. I may have appeared happy, smiley even, and perhaps I was, but I never felt joyful. Joy feels abandoning, free and uninhibited. I didn't feel free, I felt restricted. I was still holding on to the pain so tightly for fear of losing control that I was stopping myself from accessing joy. Looking back, 'joy' had a lot of shame attached to it. Happy was acceptable. I could be happy for someone else, happy to be with family, happy to be being looked after. But joy? Joy somehow felt like a betrayal, disrespectful.

There's a very strange internal conflict when you are grieving. People say they desperately want you to feel better. They tell you they can't wait for you to 'feel good again'. But we've all heard the comments from those around us who make a judgement on when they deem it proper to begin a new relationship.

The children who can't accept that their parent has met someone else. The bitchy comments on social media when someone looks as though they're having too much fun! It all filters through and the prevailing message is: 'You're allowed to move on, but only in a way that we all deem respectable and acceptable.'

My response to that is unprintable, but what I can say is we all have a very personal journey through grief. No one person has the exact same path, and grievers should never be made to feel that joy is no longer available to them. We are entitled to experience the whole gamut of human emotions. It is a very British and archaic notion that grievers should be quiet and solemn until all around them see fit to allow them to come into the light.

The danger with this is that we sometimes forget how to come back into the light. It breaks my heart when I hear people say that they don't think they can ever feel happiness again. When Matt died I thought happiness had been removed from my life for ever, but I had to stop and ask myself: 'In the two years you spent with Matt, did you ever feel unhappy?' The answer was, of course, yes. So if I'd felt unhappy when Matt was alive, then how could I believe that only his existence could make me feel happy again? It's a question of optics obviously, but the interrogation of the thought and the idea that

My dad, Colin Halfpenny,
in his younger years.

My lovely mam,
Maureen Halfpenny.

From left to right:
Paula, Dad, baby me, Nicola.

From left to right: Auntie Joyce, Nicola, my cousin Joanne (in the pink dress), my dad, and me on his lap (in the blue). This would have been taken around 1976.

Me with Mam and Dad on Christmas morning, 1978.

This photo was taken around 1979. On the left is my sister Paula,
I'm in the middle, and on my right is my sister Nicola.

Me, aged five.

Me with my stepdad, Derek, and my mam, 1983.

There were lots of happy memories. Here we are on a trip to the seaside. I'm on the left, with Nicola in the middle and Paula on the right.

With some of my drama school friends in London. I'm dressed as Busy, the maid – the part I was so disgruntled to be given!
From left to right: Lorraine, Diveen, me, Melissa.

These are some of my favourite photos of Matt and me together.

Matt was so great with Harvey, though they did have their funny moments. The image below is from the dinner when Harvey locked eyes with Matt and defiantly spat out his pudding.

With my new partner, Ian, who I met in 2023.

something has been completely removed from us is what keeps us in a constant state of deprivation.

If you do experience any moments of real joy after loss like this then I am so happy for you. It means you have kept your heart open and that you understand that feeling joy doesn't and never will take away any sorrow you have for your loved one. Remember, we are brilliant, complex human beings and we are capable of feeling many things all at the same time.

If you are yet to feel joy, that's OK too. I want to help you and give you some suggestions that may enable you to feel joyful and not like you are betraying the one you loved.

Every day, remember and repeat these four statements:

1. I am not only one thing. I can find happiness and joy in my life and still feel sad about my loss.
2. My loved one doesn't need me to be sad to be loyal.
3. I can only access my joy if I release my pain and I love myself enough to do the work necessary.
4. The best way to honour my person is to live my life with gratitude.

Two years after Matt's death, I returned to a place in Ibiza called Es Canar. Myself, Matt and Harvey had holidayed there with my sister and her family a few years before. I wasn't sure how I would feel or if it was a good idea to return but we all went back together. I remember waking one day and feeling incredibly peaceful. My head felt clear and the world felt promising and less scary. I was sat in a cafe on a beach where Harvey and Matt had played together. I was eating breakfast and I felt completely embodied by calmness. This calmness allowed a sense of well-being to enter my body and I felt joy. Joy to be alive and a strong sense that everything was going to be OK. I remember telling my sister how good I felt and she looked at me with surprise and relief. I felt secure, protected, loved, and very, very safe. A few days later I was back feeling anxious and a little down but instead of getting frustrated I held on to the fact that for a day or two I had felt a real sense of hopefulness that I hadn't been able to access for a couple of years. I told myself that I was capable of feeling that again and again and that it by no means diminished any feelings I had for the loss of Matt.

Feelings of dread, catastrophizing

Six months or so after Matt's death I was walking to Harvey's school for pick-up. I stared in horror – the school gates were shut and an air ambulance was landing in the playground. My heart immediately began to pound. I felt sick and became convinced something terrible had happened to him. I immediately asked if anyone knew what was going on. It transpired that some poor older lady had been involved in a road accident and she needed air lifting. The nearest place to land was my son's school. I felt terrible shame when the relief ran through my body on hearing it wasn't Harvey. And then I started to imagine the poor lady's family and what would happen if she didn't survive, all the pain and suffering they would go through. Which then took me to the terrible familiar conclusion that the world is scary and unsafe and bad things really do happen every day.

Now I understand that there are accidents every day and many people do die under all sorts of circumstances on a daily basis, but to live *in* that feeling, to attach myself to that thought kept me in a state of hyper-vigilance and constant fear.

This is no way to live and it only gets in the way of our healing, but we convince ourselves it's doing the opposite. If we stay ready for catastrophe then we will be more prepared, we will be able to protect our hearts, right?

Of course we can't!

Instead, like me with the air ambulance, we end up living in such a heightened state that our lives become an assault course with potential disaster at every corner. This is where the heart wants to keep building those walls. To make sure it's safe. But it's unsustainable. The paradox, as always here, is we need to lean towards vulnerability. We need to accept that life can bring us great pain and great joy in equal measure.

In order to bring about a sense of calm, I had to say this to myself every day: 'Jill, if you truly believe that bad things can happen because life is so unpredictable, then you *have* to believe the opposite is also true. You simply can't have it one way.'

Having it only one way would defy the law of physics. Push and pull, yin and yang, darkness and light, good and evil. Whichever way you want to think about it, we know that every action has its equal opposite reaction. It's a mistake to fall into the trap of thinking we are being punished in some way or, as I did for some time, that we are cursed. Grief leaves us so vulnerable that we can start to believe that life will always feel this bad. It takes time and work to stop thinking we are on some battleground. This is easier said than done, and there are still many days when I can slip into this debilitating way of thinking. If you're there too, don't worry. I will explore more in the coming chapters about ways to approach this together with other things that have helped me.

One last thought on grief work

I've shown you the ways in which grief can disguise itself and show up in our lives, but there are a myriad different ways our grief tries to get our attention.

If none of the above speak to you, then as you go about your week just be aware of any moments when you feel as though your reaction doesn't match the situation. Write it down if you can and repeat this for a few more weeks. You may begin to see a pattern, and once you recognize it you may find that there is something beneath this reaction. Something that is more truthful, more painful.

Once you recognize it, investigate. It may not seem obvious at first but try to keep asking questions. We are excellent at avoiding anything that feels too uncomfortable. It's very easy for us to think: *No, that's got absolutely nothing to do with my loss so therefore I don't have to face it.*

Our grief never goes away. If we tend to it, the space around it becomes more comfortable and more capable of gratitude and joy. If we don't, the space becomes more claustrophobic and uncomfortable.

Grief work is a gift and if you are prepared to walk through the door into the uncomfortable and the unknown you will be amazed at what is waiting for you. I promise.

How my grief work began to show up

In 2018 I was offered a role in the BBC1 drama *Dark Money*. Lewis Arnold was directing and I would be starring alongside Babou Ceesay. I loved them both. I had worked with Lewis before on the Channel 4 drama *Humans* and I'd had a great time. The whole process of making *Dark Money* felt creative and fun. I felt useful again, I felt challenged, and I felt alive! We were a real team and it reminded me why I love my job so much. For a period after Matt died I didn't know if I wanted to be an actress any more. It felt pointless and trite. I thought about retraining as a grief therapist. I wanted to help people. I wanted to be around people who were dealing with difficult times. That felt real and purposeful to me. Speaking to other people who have lost, I think this is quite common. When the person you love has gone, all the other problems in life seem to feel so insignificant. I found it really hard being around conversations where people were complaining about their body or their boss or their partner. I'd be screaming inside: *At least you have a body that works. You're lucky to have a boss, and a job. I'd give anything right now to have a partner.* Of course I understand that these are all very legitimate difficulties in people's lives, but I was coming from a place of pain and my perspective was skewed. I have spent many hours talking about these very things to my own therapist. I think grief takes us into a space where it's hard to care about anything else and that's where I was for a while. It was actually a relief to come out of that space because it made me feel isolated.

My experience on the set of *Dark Money* felt like a turning point. Not because I suddenly felt happier from that moment on – far from it. What it gave me was an ability to be around other people's pain and to have a different viewpoint on it. I noticed that I could listen to their problems without judging them because the problem wasn't harsh or traumatic enough. I could meet them where they were emotionally and feel sympathy rather than judge them. I had begun to feel stronger and more hopeful and because of that I felt a softening inside of me as I began to accept this new version of myself. I started to believe there was a future for me and that I was allowed to enjoy my work. I was allowed to tell stories for a living and not feel as if it was unworthy. It didn't take away my grief but I was allowing space for hope and faith. The hope helped me see a future that was brighter, that maybe there was a place for me in the world where I felt right. And the faith? The faith helped me to believe that when this wonderful creative experience came to an end I didn't have to cry or panic as I did all those years ago. I could be grateful to have had the experience and happy in the knowledge that there would be more to come.

These were gifts that started to come my way because of my grief work, and if you too are prepared to walk through the door into the uncomfortable and the unknown, you will be amazed at what is waiting for you. I promise.

Chapter 10

Will it always feel like this?

———

The minute I begin to reconnect with others and myself, I feel a sliver of hope, and slowly I begin to see the sand glisten and poke through the darkness.

27 March 2017: sixty-eight days since Matt died.

Dear Matt,

Happy birthday. To be able to look into your eyes and kiss you on your birthday would be my greatest wish – 44 today.

Speaking of today, wow! Just when I thought things can't feel any worse along comes today. What an absolute, unbearable devastation of a day. Every fuckin minute was a drawn-out hour of torture. Like being slowly stretched on a rack. More than once I've been on my knees begging to you, Dad, anyone, anyone! To take away the goddamn pain. Matt, it's getting worse and worse and worse.

It's as if there is a hole in my soul and nothing can fill it. I want to switch off but Harvey keeps me here. Harvey keeps me alive. Harvey is my light.

Will the world ever seem OK again? The world is noisy and I'm jittery. I hate the sound of sirens. That ride we did together in the ambulance. I was so scared, my darling. I just wanted to hold you and never let you go. I couldn't get near you. I don't know how to live without you. I don't want to feel these feelings. All our dreams, our hopes, our home, our family. Gone! Gone.

One of the scariest feelings I had around my grief is that it would never change. In my darkest days there were many times where a part of me believed that it would always be like this. I'll be honest, when I read this back just now it seems dramatic and over the top but that's me judging myself. I'm not in that kind of pain any more, my grief has shifted and changed shape. I honestly couldn't understand how I could exist feeling this bad. That day was frightening, I was on my knees begging to feel better. Reflecting back, I can see that the reason I felt so much worse is because any shred of hope and faith had left me. I was blindsided by his birthday. I didn't think it would make much difference because I already felt so terrible, but I was so scared and overwhelmed it almost took me under. That day I thought I had to accept that I would feel this bad for the rest of my life.

Even though I don't know exactly how you feel right in this moment, what I do know is that it won't always be like this. Grief moves and changes shape. Sometimes it feels spiky and rough and as if there is no space in our body for anything else. Other times it becomes smoother and more manageable, and the most confusing thing for me is that I don't always know why it's changed. Some days I wake up and it feels so bleak and heavy and I can't understand it. Nothing has happened. I haven't fallen out with anyone or had any bad news in particular. It's so unsettling. What I'm sure of is that it's constantly moving and just accepting this helps me journey through it.

The thing about progress is it's not always linear and it can often feel as if we are oscillating. We can fool ourselves that grief is a one-way journey and you must always feel as though you're getting better. This is not my experience. What I have come to learn is . . .

Grief is tidal.

Imagine you're on a beach. You open your eyes and all around you is blackness. You can't see the sand for debris and tar and thick black feathers. You try to move but you can't. You're stuck. Whichever direction you try to go, you experience so much resistance that in the end you give up.

A few weeks later you find yourself back at the beach. When you open your eyes you can see a tiny bit of sand peeking through. When you try to move your feet you find you can nudge them forward. You can breathe a little easier and the sea seems enticing as you move towards it.

A week or so later you're there again. This time it's clear. The sand is glistening and the air feels pure. You begin to run towards the water as you breathe in the salty air. There's a feeling of being propelled forward by the wind on your back. It feels like hope.

It's a week or two later and you're back. Your eyes open and the beach is black again. It feels scary and uncomfortable. This time you can't see the sea because the air is thick and dark and you're finding it hard to breathe.

This is how grief feels to me. Constantly ebbing and flowing. In my diary entry below I write about sinking, having nothing left. This had come after a period of feeling a little better and I remember how scary it was to feel as though I was being taken down again.

1 May 2017

I feel terrible today. So sad. I can't do it. I can't do this. I have nothing left. I just can't keep it up. I need to go away again and just be silent. I want that so bad . . . I'm sinking and I'm scared. I want to close my eyes and sleep for a long time. Tired, so tired. Don't even have energy to write this.

You can see that I'm feeling as if I'm being smothered by it all, but my diary was a really useful way to remind myself of the movement because it proved to me that there is always change in grief and in these dark moments I would one day return to the beach feeling clearer again.

Grief feels so confusing. It moves and changes shape, colour and texture all the time. If I visualize it as a series of contractions and expansions it becomes less bewildering.

Sometimes when I open my eyes on that black beach, I feel furious. I say to myself, 'This isn't fair! I've been doing everything I know to keep me healthy and balanced. What have I done wrong?'

There are lots of things we can do for ourselves to help us walk through our changing grief and I'll talk to you about the things that have helped me, but the chaotic, confusing nature of it is all part of the process and we shouldn't feel it's our fault.

Progress can be so incremental that it's almost imperceptible. Then our critical voices come in and we say things like, 'You should be better by now' and, 'You were better last month, what's wrong with you!'

What I want to say to you is this . . . when you're back on

the beach of grief and the blackness and bleakness have returned, when you feel like you've gone back ten steps and slid down the biggest snake on the board – you haven't. Believe me. Yes, you're feeling terrible, but every day you walk through grief is a day of learning and courage. Which means every time you return to the beach you are a different person. You're a stronger person.

It doesn't always feel this way, in fact it can feel the opposite. We can only deal with so much at a time. So when we go back we are being given only that with which we can deal. We are being given the opportunity to go deeper, peel away another layer of grief and see how courageous and vulnerable we can be.

What I'm trying to say is it isn't just the same stuff returning to you time after time. Sometimes it's a new memory, or an old thought but with a new realization, and with it comes a deeper understanding of what it is to love and lose. My thoughts over the years have swung between an acute sense of pain and a feeling that no one can ever understand me and a feeling of deep connection with humanity and realizing that love and loss is all there really is. But lessons in grief rarely come to us only once. They take practice. Which is why they keep coming back like the tides and will do until we are finally at peace with them. Please don't feel disheartened by this. We are wonderful and very clever human beings. When we grieve we naturally look for an end point, a time where we will be happy and it will no longer hurt.

This was unhelpful for me. I believed if I ran fast enough I would get there quicker. Destination done!

Integration is the key. Living with it, walking through it,

making friends with it. Trying not to disconnect when the beach feels heavy and black.

In my experience, every time I pulled back and detached, it wasn't long before I began to feel isolated. I thought that by retreating I would be able to handle the ugliness better, but I ended up feeling resentful.

The minute I begin to reconnect with others and myself, I feel a sliver of hope, and slowly I begin to see the sand glisten and poke through the darkness.

So no, it won't always feel like this – it will morph and move, but what you mustn't forget is that you are also changing. You're becoming stronger and wiser, and if we allow grief to be our teacher we learn so much about ourselves. Pain comes to us in all forms but it will always teach us something. Grief, if you let it, will drop your façade; it will reveal to you your limitations, boundaries and desires because you will be stripped of all your armour. You will get to know yourself in a brand-new way and then you can build yourself back up with love and devotion. The same love and devotion we had for the person who has left us.

We have to listen to what those tides are telling us and stay curious about what's on the beach. If we do, there will be riches to find. I promise.

Chapter 11

The light gets through the cracks

———

In that moment with Polly, I could only
be my true self. I didn't have the energy
to be anything else and she made me
feel as though I didn't have to be.

Polly is in my flat. It's six months since Matt died. The tea is made and the candles are lit. We meet once a week at the moment and take turns at each other's place. We are writing together. It's a comedy about divorce, mine to be precise. When we began, divorce had been one of the hardest experiences of my life but now it pales into insignificance. We will eventually pitch the idea to Merman productions, who will option it. We are so excited, but sadly it doesn't get made. Writing has been something I've wanted to do for a while and it's brought myself and Polly even closer. She keeps telling me that we don't have to do it, not until I feel better, but I know that day will never come. Or rather I know it will come and then go and then come and then go and then come (you get the picture). I want to push forward, feel productive, but every time we meet I end up crying into my tea and not feeling at all funny or able to write!

I look up from my drink and I say, 'I feel terrible. I feel destroyed and I feel old.'

She looks at me and replies, 'And yet you've never looked more beautiful.'

I'm completely taken aback. What is she talking about? When I look in the mirror, I see blackness, sad eyes, sallow skin with no life to speak of. What does she see? What is she looking at? I never ask her, I'm too disarmed. Grief made me feel ugly inside and out. The heaviness I've spoken about seeped into the whole of me. My face, my body, my eyes, they all feel as if they are being dragged towards the floor. Looking back now, I think what Polly was referring to was my vulnerability. I wasn't able to be anything for her other than what I was. It's not often you sit opposite someone completely devoid of personal armour or walls. We're always protecting ourselves from something. In that moment with Polly, I could only be my true self. I didn't have the energy to be anything else and she made me feel as though I didn't have to be. Her comment made me feel accepted. In all manner of ways.

I couldn't believe anyone would want to even look at me, let alone enjoy what they were seeing. I felt as though, at best, all I could ask for is to be tolerated. I had nothing interesting or new or joyful to say, so why would anyone want to spend time with me other than out of a feeling of obligation? So, in my desperate state, feeling as if I had nothing to offer, I felt an enormous sense of love pour into my body.

I didn't reject it in the way we often do when someone pays us a compliment. I was totally open because I trusted her, so I was able to receive that love fully. So there I was, feeling the worst I've felt, yet feeling the love flow through me. And this is the paradox of grief.

As the famous Leonard Cohen line says, there are cracks in everything, that's how the light gets in. These cracks allow us to receive the light in so many unexpected places.

We wake up one morning and we notice how green the

leaves on the trees are. We see a child playing in the street and it looks so beautiful. We receive a smile from a complete stranger and sense that they know how we are feeling. All of this can only happen if we stay open, only then can we receive all the beauty around us without it feeling like a betrayal.

Because this is the trick grief likes to play on us. It likes to have us believe that you can only feel sad. That there is only one acceptable feeling around here and that is bereft.

Let the light in – it's beautiful, it may be momentary and fleeting but it is by no means a betrayal.

We all live in a constant state of emotional conflict. We are happy that our son is doing well at school but things with our partner are far from good. Our relationship with our parents is wonderful but we are struggling with friendships. Our lives are always in a state of flux; just as one thing straightens out another will arise. This is life, this is the way of the universe. But when it comes to grief we tend to view it as all-powerful, a trump card if you will.

It's true that there are times when it is all-consuming, but I want to talk to you about the times when it's a little quieter or the times when friends or even complete strangers will sense what we need and gravitate towards us to bring a moment of great joy or tenderness. I stayed open in that moment with Polly. It would have been easy to close my heart and dismiss her comment because that wasn't how I felt. But I allowed myself to be seen through her eyes and because of that the light came in and I felt loved. I never want you to feel bad about experiencing these moments or feeling as if you don't deserve them. We are capable of experiencing many different emotions all at the same time and yet it was pretty revelatory to me when I first began to experience this.

For so long I had lived my life with a binary notion of allowing one emotion to override my day. It was actually through recovery that I discovered that deep sadness and regret could happily live alongside joy and hope. I had been in AA for four years by the time Matt died and never was that lesson more useful to me.

Grief isn't going away. It's with us for ever, so the sooner we allow it to exist alongside all the other wonderful things the world has to offer then the sooner we can begin to look after ourselves in the way we need. And, hey, this isn't a judgement if you're not able to do that.

This is just an invitation to let you feel all the feelings that come your way. Your grief journey is yours and judgement from others – or, indeed, judgement from yourself – is not something you need to absorb.

I experienced something immediately after Matt's death that I've told very few people about because I was ashamed and confused. Which is why I want to share it with you, in case you also felt the same or you have some other shameful feeling that you are hiding. In the immediate aftermath of losing Matt, I felt an extremely strong urge to have sex. It was quite over-whelming and like nothing I've felt before.

Any scenario in which I thought about this happening seemed entirely inappropriate and yet the thought wouldn't leave me. I couldn't understand it. *How could I ever be thinking of being with someone else?! I can't share my feelings with anyone, they would be so disgusted by me.* So thank God for the internet.

I typed into the search bar and hundreds of stories came up. People feeling exactly the same way. I read that sex releases endorphins and oxytocin and, in grief, your body is so deprived of these, your libido goes into overdrive and your body craves it. I also read that, symbolically, sex is the opposite to death. It's a way to give new life. And there were many, many people who just so desperately missed and desired touch. This very much fell in line with my body feeling like it didn't belong to me and me trying to find a way back to it.

All this is to say: however weird you think you are for feeling a certain way in grief, you can bet that one of us out there has felt the same way too. We're clever beings and our bodies and brains will do anything to survive. My body was trying to make itself feel better by acquiring the chemicals it needed to feel relaxed and happy.

To be judgemental about this is to have no real under-standing of the madness of grief but, for me, I'm glad I didn't act upon it, because looking back I was nowhere near ready for that experience. It took me almost four years to be intimate with someone and I still struggled the first time. In states of high emotion it's really hard to be discerning about our thoughts, and this is where meditating, dancing and exercise helped me. They released me from overthinking.

Meditating felt like it slowed me down, gave me a chance to pause before I reacted. The gym gave my head a break so it felt clearer and calmer once I'd finished. Dancing was a way to release some big energy blocks. I don't know how to describe it other than to say that after I do it I feel as if there is more space inside me. Does that make sense? I tried to use my mind and body in ways I knew were safe for me and wouldn't end in regret, so that I could begin to hear and feel my true desires more clearly. And, as that happened, I realized that sex was only a distraction. It was a form of escape that I so desperately wanted at that moment in time. That may not be the case for you and it may be exactly what you want and need. Take the time to care for yourself and allow grief to travel through you and you will see clearly. If you kick and scream and resist then you may never hear what your true desires are.

When we allow grief to drag us down the proverbial street, then we will grab at anything to escape the pain. Anything that allows us to escape and avoid.

If you did find yourself in this space and you are waking up regretting behaviour from the night before, please don't beat yourself up. We are already hurting; we don't need any more. Just promise yourself that for the next twenty-four hours you will look after yourself as if you are the most precious thing you have. For the next twenty-four hours only, you will nourish and care for yourself in the best way you know how.

When you wake the next day, ask yourself what felt better. The pain and regret of forty-eight hours ago or the gentle care of the last twenty-four? If the answer is the latter then you know that putting pain on top of pain isn't worth it for you. The few hours of escapism pale in comparison with the regret and shame.

I was really lucky: recovery from alcoholism had taught me that I didn't have to wait until the cracks were covered over before feeling better. They were part of me and they always would be. In fact, the cracks from my grief were never meant to be gotten rid of. I just started to learn how to support them instead of hiding them.

Grief is patient, it will wait and wait and wait, but it isn't our enemy, it isn't trying to harm us. Those little bits of light making their way through the cracks of my heart, those thoughts and desires that scared me and made me question who I was – they were all little gifts. They helped me get to know who I am and, more importantly, see myself through all of you who have lost too.

Chapter 12

Get comfortable being uncomfortable

————

When it feels spiky and coarse and painful, that doesn't mean you're doing it wrong; it just means you're feeling it. And if you choose to feel all the colours of grief, then there will be a life waiting for you on the other side that is beyond what you could have imagined.

If we haven't been taught, then how do we know how to grieve? How do we learn what works for us and what does not serve us?

I was in a unique position. I had been taught to grieve for my dad by avoiding and it didn't serve me well. I knew it had been damaging and it was beginning to affect different aspects of my life. I had already begun to explore the effects of avoiding grieving in my life through personal therapy and my 12-step programme, which is why when Matt died I knew exactly what direction I was going to go in.

But you and I are different and we all need different things, right? True . . . *but* I believe that if you want to live the fullest and most fruitful life after loss then *through* it you must go. All of it. We do not get to pass Go.

Imagine an artist's palette, the full spectrum of colours. The people we are and the families we grew up with will determine which colours we feel most comfortable in. We have usually learnt from our primary caregivers which emotions are acceptable in the household and which aren't.

Some families are amazingly open and comfortable with showing their vulnerabilities; they will sit really nicely in the nurturing space of greens but may well struggle with the reds. They may feel that anger (healthy or otherwise) is not to be displayed and is unwelcome.

Other families are willing to sit in the yellows all day long, comfortable in the happiness and joy, but feel uncomfortable expressing the vulnerability of their love in the greens, or the conflict and sadness of the blues and blacks. They don't feel safe there, so the message to the family is 'be happy' even if you're not.

So when we begin to grieve and there is a tsunami of emotions coming our way, some of them are easier for us to deal with than others. Some feel familiar and others totally foreign. The latter we push away; they scare us. We're already in pain so why deal with all this other discomfort too?!

If there was one piece of advice I could pass on to anyone grieving it is this: get really, really comfortable with being uncomfortable. Don't run away from the colours that feel unfamiliar to you. They all have a place and they are trying to teach us something.

Grief can also be incredibly complicated. I'm under no illusion that sometimes we feel very conflicted about the people we lose, and to grieve them is difficult because the feelings we have surrounding them are hard to digest. Believe me, as much as I loved Matt, I've had numerous arguments with him in death about how I feel he could have done better or how he upset me. And no, I don't always win!!! Interestingly, if I give myself time and space to get quiet and slow down, I can hear him very clearly and I have a perspective that I wasn't always capable of when he was alive. I talk to a measured, wise and extremely loving version of him. The human messiness, the resentments, all of the stupid things that got in the way of our communication have all gone. He holds me accountable but he is just love – it really is that simple. Sometimes I just feel him beside me asking me if I'm OK. I was lucky that Matt's voice was so fresh in my mind when he died; I always struggled to hear Dad's and I always wished I could. But thinking and wishing never changed anything. I am learning all the time that I cannot think myself out of grief.

Love is not rational, it's visceral, so I have to allow myself to feel the whole gamut of emotions. The childlike ones, where I feel victimized; the angry ones, where I feel the world owes me; the resentful, when I feel bitter that others seem to have it so easy; and the ugly ones, when I don't want others to have the things I have lost. I'm learning not to reject any of my feelings as unwelcome or unjustified. I invite them in, investigate them and stay curious. As time moves on, I begin to see the thoughts that don't serve me well. I can begin to see a pattern and if I remain open-hearted enough I can forgive myself for letting those feelings come back. Either I can tell the young part of me to shut up or I can listen to her, let her know I understand but that I also want to learn and evolve.

Grief is so uncomfortable it makes you want to rip your own skin off. It can make even the simplest of tasks feel over-whelming and unbearable. When it feels spiky and coarse and painful, that doesn't mean you're doing it wrong; it just means you're feeling it. And if you choose to feel all the colours of grief, then there will be a life waiting for you on the other side that is beyond what you could have imagined.

And, when I say that, I'm not talking about riches and prizes.

I mean something that you haven't experienced or even thought of for yourself before.

In those early years after losing Matt, I could not have imagined my life as it is now. I believed a life without him would be empty and consistently sad. So my life today is way beyond that, because all that I had been able to imagine was a lifetime of the discomfort I'm talking about.

Reading this, you may well be thinking, 'But why, Jill? Why should I be uncomfortable! Isn't the point of grieving to do everything in your power to make yourself feel better?'

Well, yes, we do want to feel better, but the things we have to do first will feel counter-intuitive.

As the years roll by it will be harder for us to admit that we are still in the depths of despair, because we haven't practised using the muscles we need to grieve fully. Yes, practise! I know it doesn't sound like a word we would use in conjunction with grieving. But it will all make sense. I'm still learning why it's so important to put myself back together with the utmost care.

Chapter 13

The grief retreat

I feel free, I feel safe, I feel hopeful. By
the end of the week, I feel alive!

Dear Matt, I'm sat in the doctor's surgery, it's 9.30 a.m. and I leave for the grief retreat today. I can't tell you how bad I felt this morning. Physically, yes (that's why I'm at the docs) but mentally too! I feel totally disconnected from myself. The fact that I'm off to a grief retreat because you have died is stranger to me now than it was even yesterday. I feel like my life has taken a bizarre dystopian turn and gets more confusing every day. I have to go, the doctor is calling my name.

I learnt some very valuable lessons in my first year. A friend of Polly's had attended a grief retreat in Sussex after losing a child and strongly recommended it. It was a five-day programme that offered people time, space and the tools to grieve. I had never heard of anything like it and the idea of being with a bunch of strangers for five days while we all shared our pain seemed horrific to me. I was in no mood to be around strangers.

The lady who ran the course was called Donna Lancaster and she also offered 1–1 therapy. I was way more attracted to that idea and was adamant that the retreat was not for me. However, after spending what could only have been fifteen minutes on the phone to Donna, she had somehow managed to convince me that the retreat would be a great idea! Not by being persuasive or pitching me a hard sell. Quite the opposite. She spoke with such calmness and understanding. She told me that the 1–1 was indeed available to me but she had worked in this area for many years and the power of group healing had never ceased to amaze her. She spoke to me in a way that I knew she had experienced great loss too. No platitudes or clichés, just an honest, open and gentle conversation.

So, nearly three months after Matt's death, I decided to join a group of strangers who, unbeknown to me, would change my life.

The Bridge Retreat is so named because by the end of the week we will have made the crossing over to a new way of seeing things. A reimagining. It's taking place in a large stone farmhouse in the Dorset countryside. Donna arrives and I immediately feel relief. I know I'm in good hands. She radiates warmth, strength and a tiny slice of mischief. She has beautiful caramel skin and brown eyes that sparkle through her glasses. When she smiles it feels like an invitation to be in her world.

Donna seems to have something that I want . . . peace of mind! I don't want you to think she floats around on some sort of pink cloud, she doesn't, and she would hate to be described that way too. Donna knows herself, she knows who she is in all her shadows and lightness. Her inner work shines through her like a firework, in her open face and her raucous laugh. I can sense her integrity and the fact that she wears her flaws and scars with a lightness that can only come from having done her own grief work.

I am staying in a beautiful room. It's cosy and it looks out over the gardens. The linen is white and crisp and the house has a gorgeous smell wafting through it as supper is being prepared. We've been asked to hand in all electronics; my family know where I am and they have the number so I can relax knowing they can contact me if needs be. The idea of not having my phone fills me with relief. Right now I want silence. I want to go to sleep and hunker down, but we have supper and there are a lot of new people to meet. I chat to a woman who has lost her husband in terrible circumstances. My heart aches for her, she is courageous, funny, plucky and has a beautiful soul. Her name is Emma.

The next five days are spent exploring our losses. From the very first ones in childhood up until now. I feel free, I feel safe, I feel hopeful. By the end of the week, I feel alive!

Those five days, they were transformative. They helped me open up my body and mind to be able to access the grief that was suffocating me. The handing in of our phones was so we would stay alone with ourselves, in all of the discomfort, sorrow and eventually the joy.

I was given a space to live where all we had to do was focus on our losses. Through a series of many different experiences and exercises we were given an opportunity to understand our grief. This is where I learnt that we grieve for many different things. Loss of job, loss of hope, loss of home, loss of financial security, loss of career, and on and on it goes. The tools that I discovered to help me process the people I have lost have enabled me to heal my loss of hopes and dreams too.

We were given the opportunity to look back to our very first loss and how that had affected our relationships and our outlook on life.

Your first loss can have a profound effect on how you receive the others that will inevitably come your way. Donna opened up my understanding of what loss means and how it can come in many different forms. Our first experience often comes from our parents and it doesn't have to be a bereavement. It can be grief for a relationship with them that didn't always give you what you needed. Parents who were absent a lot, emotionally or physically. Parents who demanded a lot but never gave you the space or permission to just be you.

I had been aware of my core beliefs since I was a lot younger, one of them being a fear of abandonment. As an actor you draw on these experiences and try to make sense of what kind of impact they have had on your beliefs about yourself and your surroundings. But on the retreat, I began to see how much I had been driven in some way or other by these thoughts. Those very first feelings of abandonment had seeped into feelings of rejection in relationships, the need to please with authority figures, and accepting behaviour for myself and from others that was misaligned with who I really was. These examples may all look different but are fundamentally about me wanting to feel loved and not be rejected. The lesson of learning that a core belief can keep showing up but look different was really illuminating.

All these early experiences have an enormous effect on our lives, whether we believe it or not.

Some of you reading this may have struggled, for example,

with your parents always needing you to be something other than just yourself. This results in difficulty with self-worth and pushing yourself to a point of burnout only to find an emptiness on the other side. Core beliefs form in early childhood and influence how we see the world and who we are. At the retreat we discussed these core beliefs, challenged them, had empathy for the inner child that bought into them, and understood how they were or were not serving us.

It's hard for me to fully explain the journey I went on there, but looking back at my diary entries from that time, I'm talking to Matt and I tell him about the 'wonderful healing time I've had'. I left the retreat with hope. Hope that I could cope. Hope for my future and hope for the person I was becoming. I called my mam at the station when I was travelling back home. She couldn't believe how different I sounded. Not just what I was saying but my voice itself. It had a lightness to it, and that was because for the first time since Matt died I was starting to believe that life wouldn't feel this bleak for ever.

Some of the things I learnt at the grief retreat I have carried with me and integrated into my life. As I write this today, I have received some news about my son's health that I feel really sad about. I am worried for him and I want more than anything for him not to have to experience this. Instead of staying with the facts and the next possible steps *and* the sadness, I have managed to add into the mix thoughts like 'of course this has happened – just as things felt as though they were going in the right direction, this comes along! To bring me back down to earth and remind me to never get too happy!'

Now I know this is untrue. There isn't a big bad witch lurking in the background waiting to punish me just as I begin to feel joyful about my life, but there is an old belief I have: 'the fairy-tale curse'. The girl who is doomed never to be happy. This has been formed in childhood, by trauma. The trauma itself and the way the trauma was dealt with mean I go to this place when I feel scared and overwhelmed. Thankfully, experiences like the grief retreat have given me the ability to see that trauma response, have sympathy for the little Jill who is scared for her son and feeling out of control, but also to hold the adult part of her alongside the child. The part that tells me it's natural to worry about my son. I am not cursed. Life happens and there are twists and turns but I am not being punished because I am a bad person.

It may seem difficult to comprehend how we tie this into our grief but that is why loss can feel so utterly despairing. It is not only the situation itself we are mourning but all of the long-held belief systems we carry along with us.

The experience of the grief retreat helped me realize that grief is a process that requires patience and time and that there are things we can do to help ourselves to heal.

I learnt that grief comes to visit at unexpected times and as my life moved on and work began to pick up I was aware more than ever how it could catch me off guard. I never woke up on a morning and thought, *This is the day when it will all unravel.* It seemed to sneak up on me when I least expected it and when I was doing something I'd done hundreds and hundreds of times before. One such day was five months after Matt's death.

I'm not feeling great, but an audition has come through for a play and part that I'm drawn to. I've done so many auditions over the years and putting any personal situations aside is something all actors are excellent at. The row you've just had with your partner or the sad news you've just received from a friend will rarely enter the room unless we feel we can use the energy for what we need. Today is no different. I have a job to do and that is to go into the room, have an obligatory chat, then get into the reading I've been asked to prepare. I am feeling vulnerable and raw but I've hidden my feelings so many times I don't even question it.

The material I have to read is about a woman who is feeling extremely disillusioned with her life. She is depressed and angry (I can relate!). The director and I have the mandatory exchange, full of questions that neither of us are really interested in knowing the answer to:

'Did you get here OK? Far to travel?'

'It's hot, isn't it?'

Then another question, one that I'm sure he doesn't really want the answer to but feels he has to ask.

'So how are you?'

What I usually say is 'Good, thanks' or 'Fine, you?' Today something different happens. I suddenly realize that I don't have the energy to pretend. I can't bring myself to lie, it all just feels so pointless. I tell him exactly how I am AND I tell him why. I cry and then I'm so embarrassed I want to run away.

There's an awkward pause, he asks me if I'm OK to read and I say, 'Yeah, of course.' After I've finished, he tells me I was great. I feel shame rushing through my body. I can't imagine why anyone would want to begin a four-month theatre job with a person who is so obviously struggling. We say our goodbyes and I leave.

I didn't get the job, but that's not the point of this story. I should have called my agent that day and told them I wasn't up to it. I'm sure I could have rescheduled. I needed to be alone and to allow myself to be where I was. But as life moves on at its usual fast pace we can feel pressure to run alongside it when what we really need is to put on the brakes. I really wanted to get the job. I wanted to work, I wanted to feel creative, I wanted to be somebody else for a couple of months. I could dress this up in any way that suits. I could argue that it's my job and I needed to earn money. I could tell you how much creativity releases me from difficult feelings, but ultimately the retreat had taught me that maybe I just needed to be quiet and be on my own. It was also a great reminder of the non-linear journey through grief. My time in Leeds before this had been wonderful, why wouldn't it be the same now? Why did I feel worse? Because that's where I was at and the point for me was not to judge it but to accept it.

It seemed that the times grief would overwhelm me were when I knew I had to stay in control, like the audition. Basically any time my brain would tell me that it was necessary to be *in* control, I would get a surge of feeling out of control. I would give myself a little pep talk to be able to get through the next moment. And I did, many times. But if I continue on with my day and do all the things I need to do before bed, then where does that squashed feeling go? What will I be holding on to and what happens to my body and my brain?

A lot of people find it really difficult to take time out for themselves. A typical response would be, 'I get up, feed the kids, do the school run, go to work, come back home, and repeat.' By the time the weekend arrives they are exhausted and that's before the kids' activities or plans with friends etc., etc. But what would happen if you scheduled your grieving? This was something I began to think about after the grief retreat. We discussed setting aside time for ourselves. I did it with everything else in my life, but how would I feel if I did it to grieve? What would that even look like? Putting thirty minutes aside a few times a week to grieve? I know what you're thinking: 'That's stupid! How do I know when I'm gonna feel sad or when I'm gonna be thinking about them?'

What I'm suggesting here is that there are occasions in our week when we know we can be in a safe place at home, in a park or our car, when we can dedicate time towards thinking about our loved one. We don't have to sit and cry, we might want to listen to a favourite song of theirs, remember some special times we had or look at photographs. Whatever it is, it is time dedicated to our person, where we allow ourselves to feel whatever we want without thinking we have to suppress or hide it. So all those moments throughout the week where we swallow and push down have a place to breathe and permission to be with us in that allotted time. It may seem like an alien concept to schedule your grief but if we don't, weeks can often fly by without us giving ourselves any time to decompress. The feelings are swirling around our body and we are barely holding on. So if you relate to the feeling of having no time, then schedule a slot in your week and make it yours. Ten, twenty, thirty minutes, whatever you've got. Give it to yourself. Don't be tempted to do the washing or answer emails or anything else that may be on your to-do list. Just be with your loved one and let yourself know that this is your time for each other.

Chapter 14

How to take time out to grieve

The grief work may feel challenging and taxing, but the idea of being stuck again (as I was as a child) was way more frightening.

There's no one way to work through grief. I've tried lots of things over the years and I'd like to share with you some I have found to be helpful. A few I picked up from the grief retreat or from AA recovery, others are things I've read in books or that have been recommended by friends. They don't take up a lot of my time and I vary them according to how I feel or what I need on that day. Over time, they have helped me feel differently about the way I carry my grief – I hope that some of them might help you too.

Walking

I am walking alone in the grounds of the grief retreat. We have been invited to go out and bring back anything that catches our eye, anything that moves us or touches our heart. I find myself looking in a different way from usual. It's concentrated and I linger on what I see, taking in nature and all its glorious colours and shapes. I realize how little I do this back home. How little time I give to the beauty around me. How my appreciation of nature is fleeting and I forget to stay with it. It feels bliss to only have this to do.

The simplicity of the task slows me down. I feel calm. My mind wants to tell me this is all a bit stupid and how the hell is this gonna fix anything, but my body tells a different story. I can't deny that the sense of calm right now is helping me remember who I am. The person I am without the stories to tell. I have a sense of travelling back towards myself.

I choose a small rock. It has a gorgeous dark pattern inscribed inside it. I decide it will be the piece I take back to the group. When we reconvene, we chat about what we found, why we chose it and what if anything it reminds us of. It's the simplest and gentlest of exercises and yet it centres me. It makes me feel small again, like a child finding pebbles on the beach to show her mam. It reminds me that joy can be found in the most basic of tasks and it is all around us, always, we just have to take the time to look.

After leaving the retreat, I took the experience of the walking exercise and turned it into a practice. I have found it's helpful to get specific. My best walks are always the ones where I am paying attention.

I'd encourage you to try this yourself. Walk with an intention. tell yourself you will choose something to take back home with you. Anything wild from nature that brings you joy. If it helps, imagine it as an offering for your loved one. Something you're bringing back for them.

Try walking to a favourite spot of yours or your loved one. Somewhere that holds a special place in your heart. Tell them where you're going before you leave and journey with them. Keep them alongside you as you walk and stay as close as possible to them in your heart. In my mind we are going together. I am not visiting somewhere without them, I'm visiting somewhere with them in a different form. This is very personal and, whatever your beliefs, it may not work for you, but for me it puts a whole different spin on the journey. I feel very certain that my loved ones are beside me in spirit. I can sense their energy and it brings me comfort to think this way. When I feel open and connected I feel a force field of love around me. It's visceral for me, but if this isn't something you can connect to then that's more than OK. Bring them along in memory, put a photograph in your pocket if it helps. We are all so different and it doesn't matter what our beliefs are about afterlife. Grieving is universal.

Walk in your favourite environment. It doesn't matter if this is forest, sea, urban or residential. All that matters is it's somewhere that brings you peace. Grief is tiring; being around a place that relaxes us helps to calm our nervous system.

For me it's the sea. I feel very calm around water. It gives me perspective and I find it soothing. I feel less alone. As I look out to the water I can imagine the millions of us who have loved and lost and how we are all trying to find our way. It makes me feel connected to you all and to myself. It fills me with life. I love to watch the waves crashing against the sea wall as much as I love to see the paddleboarders and the dippers. Find your happy spot and go to it as much as possible. Think about why you like it and allow yourself to feel inspired by it. Do you love the architecture of the city you're in? Do you love to wander around the town where you grew up and think of all the people you have encountered? Do you love the trees in the forest and how insignificant they make you feel?

One of the joys I have found with walking in nature is the changing seasons. Watching the flowers grow wild in the forest in springtime then to be gone in a few months as the summer comes to an end and autumn creeps in. It mirrors the changing faces of grief. The seasons bring me a clear sense of time. As someone who thinks that everything they ever did was 'a few weeks ago' or 'a couple of years back', the seasons give me a clear timeline. They remind me of my progress and they tell me to slow down. That my feelings are ever-changing and will continue to be. The shedding of autumn reminds me that the braver I am about letting go of some of my long-held beliefs that hold me back, the lighter I will feel and the braver I will become. The winter teaches me that the rawness I have felt in grief is necessary. Being stripped back to my essential being and feeling as though I have no armour is what softens me and humbles me. I can slow down and take stock. The budding of spring lets me see very clearly that renewal is possible, that I am allowed to feel better and if I don't, then not to worry, as change is always happening whether I can feel it or not. And the summer with all its colour and bloom reminds me that I can be happy and light-hearted while also holding my sadness alongside me. The seasons are a stark reminder that life really does go on and as the years go by this feels less scary and more comforting to me.

Things will shed and renew year after year and that's what we will do. We will continue to shed and to grieve and to make way for new life and new energy to enter, only to feel we are being stripped away again. However we feel in this moment is not how we will feel for ever. The seasons teach us that the pace at which we live our lives and the pace at which we expect ourselves to 'get better' is unrealistic. Listen, watch and move through the seasons, knowing that each of your years will be filled with beautiful moments full of colour and verve coupled with a stripping away and a feeling of shedding. If we accept this will be what our time on earth looks like, then we won't be so disappointed by unfulfilled expectation.

Gratitude

I used to live my life feeling like there was a 'destination happiness'. I would say things like, 'When I'm thirty-two, I won't feel this way about my career, my body or my love life. I'll be in my home with my family and everything will feel sorted.' That just hasn't been my reality and I can't imagine it's anyone's really. There are so many unforeseen incidents in life that either delight us or take us under, which is why it's so important to live presently. I know, I know, that phrase again. The one everyone tells us we have to do, yet most of us don't know how! My experience with grief has forced me to live presently. Honestly, on some of my darkest days I lived minute by minute, never mind day to day. It made me look at what was in front of me that very moment instead of what I had lost. I had to, in order to survive.

For example, thoughts of how I was going to get through Matt's birthday or my first Christmas without him were too much to bear and incredibly debilitating. Sometimes I would sit in a cafe with a cake and cup of tea and think to myself: *For these next ten minutes I have something nice to eat and drink; I will get through these ten and then I will deal with the next ten after that.* Anxiety is all about the future, what might happen, how will something feel, what could it look like? We never really know what's round the corner, but grief highlights this so acutely. So what I tried to do whenever possible was to stay in the moment and practise gratitude.

For some years now I have written a gratitude list. I first heard about this practice in my 12-step programme. I list ten things each night that I am grateful for and I send the list to three people, who send me theirs back. At first I was worried that I wouldn't be able to think of two things, let alone ten each day. And why would I feel grateful when I was feeling wretched?! Just believe me when I say it works.

There are no rules about what you can put on your list – and nothing is too big or too small. On my worst days in the very early weeks after losing Matt, where the struggle felt unbearable, my list would include things like:

> *I am grateful that I was able to get out bed and take Harvey to school.*
> *I am grateful that I have money to look after us.*
> *I am grateful that I didn't break down in the supermarket.*

What this enabled me to do was focus on the smallest of things and realize that there were indeed many ways in which my days could have been worse. It's so easy when we are experiencing deep pain to bunch our whole day together and just say 'it was terrible', because that *is* how it feels. It's a very simple but effective exercise to challenge yourself to break your day down and see where there is gratitude to be had. It can be as small-seeming as you like – a cup of tea, an episode of your favourite show, a magazine. As time goes on you will find it easier to see those moments as your day unfolds.

At other times my gratitude list can feel very intense and profound. It may read:

> *I'm grateful I survived this morning when I felt like I was going under.*
> *I'm grateful my sister picked up the phone when I was feeling so afraid.*

It doesn't matter what's on there; what matters is that you can look for the moments to be grateful and to understand that gratitude is powerful. I feel empowered if can find things to be grateful for when I am in a state of despair. It helps me to believe I can survive.

A meditation I came across some time ago from the Stoics has helped me through some dark days. I totally appreciate it may not be for everyone but it has been a gift for me.

The practice is called negative visualization. The idea is that we focus on something that is extremely upsetting to us, something that we hope will never happen. Once we have the feeling inside us of this truly terrible occurrence, we can then focus our minds and go into our meditation feeling unbelievably grateful that it hasn't happened.

Now you might baulk at this and think, 'Jill, that's a hideous idea, taking ourselves to a place of despair just to be grateful that it hasn't happened.' Personally, I think it's incredibly powerful. It's a stark reminder that things could always be worse and a reason to be happy in that moment.

On my worst days where I couldn't see any light, I would sometimes imagine losing my family. The pain and terror of that thought was so acute that once I could tap into the gratitude of them still being here, I suddenly felt a rush of happiness that they were alive and well.

Of course this must be done properly and we need to make sure you get to the end of the meditation where you are feeling deep gratitude. We don't want to get stuck in the negative thoughts and not be able to move out of it. As I said, this is a difficult concept and it may not be for you.

Some of you may be thinking, 'Of course I'm glad my child/ mother/partner is alive, that's obvious.' But for others reading this book, that loss will be our reality and we will wonder why we didn't wake up every morning and thank the universe that this person was still with us.

Once we have lost someone, if we allow ourselves to be grateful we will begin to see the beauty in the world everywhere. Suddenly a pleasant encounter with a server at your local coffee shop or a kind assistant on the other end of the phone will mean the world to you.

When my world was blown apart by Matt's death, it felt scary and hostile and yet I was also exposed to some of the gentlest and kindest acts of human nature. Acts that I would have no doubt taken for granted before. These days, those moments I encounter are little gems that I can hold inside me and know that they will be appearing on my gratitude list that evening. The best portrayals of this feeling of gratitude are in the movies *It's a Wonderful Life* and *A Christmas Carol*. Both films capture the spirit of what it might be like to see life differently. The protagonists are both offered an opportunity to look at their circumstances and re-imagine them. The deep, deep gratitude they experience afterwards allows them to see life through a different lens.

My grief has taken me down some very dark alleys, but I am always aware that it could have been worse. If I only focus on what I've lost instead of what I have, the lens through which I see my life will be narrow and restricted. The Stoic meditation showed me through my darkest despair there was still so much to be grateful for. When I thought I couldn't feel any worse, I imagined a scenario where it was indeed worse and thought to myself, *Thank God I'm not going through that*. Which then enabled me to fill up my gratitude list without any hesitation at all! Two different approaches but the exact same intention.

Dance

My grief retreat experience gave me back the gift of dancing like nobody's watching. Not actually dissimilar to flailing around in my bedroom as a little girl, only this time I was conscious about why I was doing it. We were given the opportunity to let all the tension go and dislodge the energy inside our bodies.

The first time I did this at the grief retreat, we were in the main room. It was large enough to house all fourteen of us with plenty of space still to move. There were floor-to-ceiling glass doors with light flooding through them at one end and a sound system at the other. Even though all that was required of us was to move, I think many of us were nervous about this exercise. It's hard to dance like no one is watching; it feels vulnerable and a little embarrassing. The music was turned up really loudly. We started off gently at first, swaying our bodies from side to side, warming up as we tried to let the music inform us. The speakers blared and I began to move more, safe in the knowledge that any screams or wails that left my body would go unheard. As the drums grew louder my body moved and shook and stomped. I closed my eyes and allowed myself to let go. The more I let go, the more I wanted to. I could feel the energy shift and all sorts of visions and colours were appearing before my eyes. Eventually I opened them and still allowed myself to move with complete abandon. Even though I didn't look at anyone else, I could sense an unlocking and discharging all around me. At the microphone, Donna encouraged us all to let go and just allow. She was our hype woman and it was fantastic!!! The anger was moving around my body, the sadness was seeping out and the joy was moving in. It's really, really hard to dance for a period of time this way and not start to feel slightly euphoric. It's a literal release and releasing feels so good.

This anger is a huge part of my grief. Like a rage against the world and all the unfairness in it. And a lot of it is really un-attended sadness and feelings of abandonment. But although my anger has worked in many ways as motivational fuel in my life, propelling me forward, it has diminishing returns. I know that the longer I use it the more ineffective it will become. I will have to keep adding to it to get it to work as potently as before. This is where I start to get confused and where I begin to self-sabotage. It's when I'm in danger of seeking out new relationships and opportunities to destroy so that I can add more fuel to the fire. So I need to shift it. I need to make way for a more truthful and less harmful form of motivation.

When something has been trapped inside us for a long time, talking therapy alone is often not enough. Trauma gets stuck in our bodies. The energy of holding on to our pain means the body has to work very hard to carry all that extra weight around. Many of us will never relate the pain in our body to our heartbreak, we wouldn't link a physical feeling with an emotional experience. My fear of being abandoned lived inside my body as a child and manifested itself as anxiety. I didn't have the words to express it or even know it. All I had was a feeling, an energy that lived inside me. And that energy needed to move and shift. My dancing lessons helped me enormously but my dancing at the retreat was on a different level. I wasn't being asked to have a straight back or think about technique, in fact I was being actively encouraged to let it all go. To be free. To release! It felt fantastic, to be free from rules. To not care what I looked like, to know I wouldn't be judged. It was purely for me. It left me feeling amazed at the power of movement, and it's absolutely something we can all do.

First choose a room in your home where you can have privacy, where you won't be worried about noise or disturbances. Wear headphones if that's appropriate.

Next choose some music that stirs you, something that speaks to your body. For me it would be tribal music with some pretty intense drums. I prefer not to move to vocals as they distract me, but you choose whatever you like. Make sure there is enough playtime to last for the time you've scheduled in, or if it suits you play the same tune on a loop.

Before you start to dance, allow yourself to connect to your feelings. Your anger may feel very specific or a general rage. You might not even feel angry; you may feel numb or stuck. Our energy blocks will be different in all of us. Take a few minutes to think about it and allow your body to feel. If it's non-specific, simply tell your body that it doesn't need to hold on to anything that isn't serving it any more. If it's a specific incident/person, you can say out loud that you are letting it go as it doesn't serve you.

If you feel a little lost, then you can start by shaking. Shake your hands in front of you (as if you're drying them), take them high above your head and then down below your waist. Imagine you are shaking something out of you.

Then do the same with your feet and legs. Go to your neck and your shoulder joints and get them moving until your body begins to wake up and feel warm. Then all you need to do is move. Move and stomp and shake and stamp in whatever way makes you feel good, and off you go.

Every couple of months or so I will give myself some time to lock myself in my bedroom, turn up the music and off I go. When I do it I keep going until I feel pretty exhausted. It can take me a while to really let go and start to release, but once I do it feels amazing. By the time I'm finished I'm tired and discharged. I feel lighter and freer. The time you take is your choice but try to keep going until you're really tired.

It's a great way to allow the energy flow back through our bodies. To dislodge the blockages and reset. You may feel strange at first; you may struggle to let go and really move your body with abandon. That's OK. Keep trying and, remember, no one can see you. This is for you and you alone. It's private.

If you give it a go and you don't like it or get anything from it, that's OK. Don't beat yourself up, don't think you've failed. There are other ways to move . . .

Exercise

I wasn't sure if I would be able to return to the gym where Matt had collapsed but I found myself back there and in the spin studio within weeks. It may sound strange, but I wanted to be back in the room where he was last alive. I wanted to imagine him in the class. I would take a bike at the back of the studio. It was a windowless room and the lights were low so the room was dark. The music would be blasting and the instructor would be shouting her instructions into her microphone. I would cry as I cycled, staring at the floor where I had watched the paramedics use the defibrillator, and I would feel so angry and confused about why he had gone. At the end of the class I'd wipe my face with a towel and off I'd go.

Seems a little mad when I write it down, but it's what I wanted to do so I did it. It obviously gave me what I needed until it didn't. One day I decided I didn't want to go to the class any more and that was that. What I did know, though, was that I still needed to exercise.

I've been working out in some way or other since I was a little girl. From those early years when I danced, all through my drama school days and into early adulthood. I always knew I needed exercise, especially when I was out of work. I used to think I was only working out for my body; now I realize it was my head that needed it more. Grief interrupts our system and the stress it puts on us physically means that even if exercise is the last thing you feel like doing it will always be beneficial. Releasing endorphins can help relieve the stress we are under. We just need to find the one that works best for us, so don't be afraid to experiment.

In my early days of losing Matt, I noticed a huge decrease in my energy levels and my strength. What had been pretty easy for me now felt like a struggle but I intuitively knew why. Try not to be disheartened if you too have a drop in performance. Know that your body is healing and a huge amount of energy is being taken from you each day to cope with the pain you're in. Just keep going, stay as consistent as possible and lower your expectations of yourself. I tried to let my body dictate to me what it wanted to do.

Yoga calms me down and helps to regulate my nervous system while also challenging my body. The interesting thing about yoga is it's all about where you are at that day, that moment. The philosophy behind it is to know when to go to your edge and when to pull back. To figure out what your body is asking of you that day. In this sense, it was the most challenging exercise for me. My grief and my ego were in battle. Yoga very much held a mirror up to me about where I was at and what I was prepared to accept of myself. It's also a lesson in breathwork. We are asked to follow the breath with each move we make and try to connect our mind and body so we move as one. My favourite yoga classes where I have been able to achieve this have felt extremely meditative.

I attended a yoga class only a week or so after Matt died. I went along with my sister Nicola; we were both in need of moving our bodies and she knew how much I was struggling and feeling disconnected. I remember doing maybe only two thirds of the class. I felt exhausted and emotional. I lay on the mat as the class continued in a pose known as shavasana, otherwise known as corpse pose. You lie on your back with arms down, palms facing up and legs flat and relaxed. It's a restorative position and how most yoga classes end. I had enjoyed moving and getting back into my body but I knew I needed to stop. As I lay there I could feel the tears running down my face. I let them. I knew I was in a safe place. As the class came to a close and rest of the students joined in shavasana, I felt my sister's hand hold mine. We lay together and cried, knowing the journey we were facing. I've been in yoga classes where someone has lain on the mat for the whole session; it's where they're at and there is no judgement around that. A good yoga class will have an atmosphere of release and freedom and just being around that energy can feel incredibly soothing.

As time moved on I began to enjoy strength-based exercise. Maybe that was because I felt a lot of my strength had left me and I wanted to build it back up. I began to lift smaller weights and liked that fact that I felt stronger quite quickly. These days I'm enjoying Olympic weightlifting. I started when I moved back to Newcastle in the summer of 2019. There's something about lifting a barbell from the floor to above your head that feels strangely powerful. Some of the women who train there are ridiculously strong and I love to watch them in their zone. It would be very easy for 'old me' to compare myself, but that's not what's it's about any more. Some days, when it's been a challenging class, I think to myself: *There were days not too long ago where I felt I could barely hold myself up, let alone a heavy bar.* It's just a really nice reminder that I am stronger than I believed. In mind and body.

Whatever kind of exercise you like and enjoy, do it! Just keep on giving your body a chance to move and to get out of your head. Don't put any judgement on what it is, only that you enjoy it. Remember, the body keeps the score. It stores the tension and the hurt, so find what works for you in order to keep releasing them. The only rule here is if it makes you feel good, then it's right. It's so personal for each of us and can be a huge mental hurdle.

Grief detached me from my body some days. I was so in my head that I almost felt like my body didn't belong to me. It would have been easy to abuse and reject it but luckily for me I had learnt that my body needs care and attention the same way as my head does. I had been fortunate enough to learn that lesson as a kid all those years ago in dance class. I know the two work together and if you neglect one you usually end up paying the cost in some way. Whatever way you look at it, you will never regret an exercise session.

Writing

There were days (and still are) when my head does not stop turning. Does this chime with you? I call it 'washing machine head'. Thoughts spin around aimlessly and I'm not able to focus on any one in particular. As I reach for one, ten others come into view and I'm distracted and confused.

What I find useful is to write something down by hand. It captures my feelings in a way that keyboards can't quite touch. I leave a pen and paper by my bed each morning and as I wake, before I reach for a phone or a tea, I write for five minutes. If you want to try this, you could set a timer if it helps. Try not to think too much about what you're writing, just let it flow as a stream of consciousness. These are what's known as morning pages and if it helps you, think of them as a brain dump.

I learnt about morning pages in Julie Cameron's amazing book *The Artist's Way*. I was in my first year of recovery and decided to give them a try. They are a chance to drop off all the unconscious thoughts and feelings that are swirling around our minds before we even get out of bed. To make way for the good stuff, the important stuff! It's a way to allow us to focus on what needs the most attention that day.

The morning pages helped me through my grief because there were a lot of thoughts invading my mind from the minute I awoke. A lot of anger, fear, hopelessness, despair. It was a deluge of the radio that played in my mind – Shit FM. Just allowing this brain dump first thing means I don't have to contend with the unhelpful thoughts later in the day. They have been diluted or even banished for the day because I have spewed them out and given them a place to reside. It feels like a five-minute workout for my mind, a clearing or sweeping away of all the thoughts that come to engulf me in the morning. If the morning isn't possible for you, then please know that this practice can be done any time of the day. Don't deny yourself because you can't do it first thing. Leave pens and paper dotted around the house and when you have time, pick them up and, without thinking, begin to write.

My pages often consisted of old ideas about myself. Old beliefs and unhelpful stories I had told myself from long ago about feelings of worthlessness. It was powerful because even though I didn't necessarily believe those thoughts any more, they were still within me, and this is the crux of the pages. We are not our thoughts, we can think a million different things throughout our day, and if someone asked us if they were an accurate reflection of who we are, we may say, absolutely not! So it's a great exercise to allow your flow of thoughts to be written down and then look back and say, 'Wow, I didn't even know I was still thinking that. Do I really believe that?' If the answer is yes then we know there is still work to be done. At other times it was a way to flush them all out and make way for my day.

In order to cope with our grief, we can turn to old ideas to distract us from our pain. Mine tended to go inward and would look something like this: *Had a bad dream last night. Dreamt that I could see Matt but he was ignoring me. I feel terrible, like I'm cursed. I don't think I'll ever meet anyone because I'm always gonna feel this sad and no one will want to be with someone who is cursed.*

I am being punished. He probably didn't even love me. Dad didn't care . . .

The truth is I did sometimes feel like that, but not all the time, and ultimately I knew it was rubbish, but when I felt my most vulnerable the feeling would become louder. The pages enabled me to write it, see it and then leave it. Dump it for the day or even for the next hour and give something else a chance to get in there.

Challenging our thinking requires strength, strength we don't always have in grief. Grief is tiring, and if our brain wins out that day it will want us to think the lazy thoughts. The easy, low-hanging fruit. But our pages allow us to give them a place outside our brain so that when we get out of bed and into the shower we can ask the questions:

How do I really feel today?
What do I need to do today to help me feel better?
What can I put in place today to allow me to have a better day?

The thoughts will no doubt come back. In fact, one of the amazing things about the morning pages is the repetition. After a month, try reading back your entries. You will no doubt be amazed at just how much repetition there is. It helps you to understand that in order to feel better we have to interrupt those patterns and give ourselves things to do that stop the washing-machine head. The purge of the thoughts in the morning pages really helps slow my thinking down for the rest of the day. Having allowed the less important or perhaps more incessant ones to have a voice, I can then give my attention to what is most relevant that day. Often my loudest thoughts are merely distractions from what is underneath – the more painful or difficult ones.

Crying

'My name is Jill and I am a crier.'

I have always felt a lot of sadness within me and I'm glad I'm able to cry. It's cathartic, a release. But from the ages of four to twenty I don't remember crying specifically about my dad. I would try sometimes and nothing would come out because I had completely disconnected myself from the event. I didn't have a problem crying to my Richard Clayderman tapes, or at the end of my *Annie* production or Zammo struggling with addiction in *Grange Hill*!!! I had simply transferred the sadness. The trauma of Dad was unattended, so my brain had to find other avenues to express it. If this chimes at all and you feel you cry very easily yet there is a way more upsetting incident in your life that you find difficult to be moved by, then it may be a similar scenario. I'm just grateful that I found other outlets.

A lot of people see crying as either something negative or something that at a certain point we stop doing because we are no longer sad enough or we have 'moved on'. It feels as if there is a time frame for what we deem acceptable in terms of tears. I hear people say, 'Oh, it's been ten years now, I don't cry about it any more.'

I think crying is brilliant. I see it as a complete release and I don't think we should be embarrassed or ashamed of it. I understand that most of us see it as an incredibly vulnerable and private act, but that seems unfair to me.

I was given some terrible advice a few days before Matt's funeral: 'Tell Jill not to speak to anyone in the crematorium until after the service, because if she does she might get upset and cry.' I mean, what kind of BS is that! I'm being advised to only cry at a certain time within the service because God forbid I lose control and actually show people how I really feel!!!! I just find the whole thing incredibly disheartening.

I hear people congratulate themselves about how they got through the whole funeral without breaking down and it was only when they finally got home that they could cry. It makes me sad that we see it as a weakness. Being your true self is brave, being vulnerable in front of others is powerful, and crying at a funeral is the most natural of reactions. I think we're taught to hide our emotions and keep them to ourselves. It's seen as undignified to 'lose control'. I see it as the opposite. I see crying as being in control of your power. You feel it and release it and are able to withstand others' discomfort with it.

That's pretty strong, if you ask me. When people ask me about my dad or Matt now, I may begin to talk and start to cry.

'I'm sorry,' they say. 'I didn't mean to make you cry.'

'You didn't,' I reply. 'It's my choice to.' And it will continue to be for the rest of my life. Our tears never run out, we merely stop giving ourselves permission.

When you exercise, you sweat; when you're in pain, you cry.

Of course people will say, 'Yeah, but it's not always appropriate to cry, you might be at work!' I'm not suggesting we walk around crying all the time, but I would like the stigma of crying to be removed and for people to stop apologizing when they do it. This is all self-care. Tending to our needs. It's easy to think that self-care has to be pleasant. A bath, a walk, a book. It can be, but if what you want to do is put on a favourite song and cry, then that's self-care too.

Letter writing

I took part in a very powerful letter-writing exercise at the grief retreat. I was given the opportunity to write a letter both to my dad and to Matt, being as open and as honest as I could, and for Donna and the rest of the group to 'witness' my letter as I read it out loud.

What this exercise enables us to do is to access our deep inner child, to let go of the rational and express core beliefs that get to the nub of the pain and grief in a way that we don't often allow ourselves. Some of us may feel uncomfortable going to these places. We have kicked that small child to the kerb so many times that we don't listen to them any more, but believe me when I say how powerful it is.

Another aspect of this exercise, which can only be done with the input of a professional like Donna, is that the professional then responds out loud to your letter. Donna worked with me to take the exercise to this level. This isn't necessary if this option isn't available to you, though. The writing and the witnessing are also very powerful.

In the first letter, I told my dad I was really angry at him for abandoning me. That he had ruined parts of my childhood because he left us with a grieving mam. I had made bad decisions because of his departure and it had affected seemingly every part of my life. In Matt's, I also told him how angry I was that he had left me so suddenly. How he had broken my heart and left me to rebuild my life again without him in it. Both letters, although different in content, had a very strong narrative of being left and feeling abandoned. Both had themes of feeling as though I had been bad and was being punished. They were full of anger and shame and they definitely came from a very young and damaged part of myself, the raw unfiltered child inside of me. The inner child is the primitive part of us that behaves and reacts in response to emotional scars. A childhood force. This was particularly poignant for me as I felt my grief had been frozen in time and the feelings were congealed inside me.

Donna responded from the 'best part' of my dad, meaning she responded from love. She (as my dad) apologized for how I felt and told me she understood why. She explained (to little Jill) that he had never wanted to leave us in pain and he loved me dearly. She did the same for Matt, and something happened that seems very obvious and simplistic, yet felt very magical.

You see, when she replied to me, I was ready to *receive* what I heard. The majority of what she said, the adult part of me already knew, but this time it *hit* differently. It landed. And that's because I was receiving it as my child self too, the wounded part of me. It needed to go there because that was the part that longed to be healed.

I had taken time to write my letters, during which it was important to be alone and uninterrupted. I chose my words carefully; it wasn't a rant, it was a clear expression. So when Donna sat opposite me and listened without interruption, I felt as though I was being really heard, maybe for the first time. Because of that I felt calm, safe and rooted in my own body. Every part of me was engaged with the exercise and I was allowing myself to respond rather than react. I heard every single word she spoke back to me and it felt as though it landed in my body. I felt totally seen.

When writing the letter, Donna encouraged us to use sentences like:

> *My experience of you was . . .*
> *What I needed from you and didn't get was . . .*
> *How I felt/feel . . .*
> *What I need you to know is . . .*
> *What I can/can't forgive you for is . . .*
> *What I need to apologize to you for is . . .*

And then anything else we wished to say before our final goodbye, a goodbye to how we had held on to them. This is a powerful symbol of our journey moving forward.

At the retreat we had professionals and ready-made witnesses, but if you're doing this at home, you will need to find a witness. A 'witness' is a trusted person in your life who will listen to your letter without trying to fix – 'Oh no, let's go out and cheer you up' – or mirror – 'Oh yeah, that happened to me too, awful isn't it?' A very trusted friend who will listen and witness and that is it. Why? We all desire to be listened to. The letter is a chance for you to say out loud all of your perhaps shameful, difficult and very private thoughts. Feelings that we know as adults don't always make rational sense but nevertheless they reside within us. Things that have happened that you may never have told anyone.

When you are ready, invite your witness to listen to you read the letter out loud. Take your time and stay present. Talk slowly, and if you begin to get upset, take your time to breathe and get the words out as clearly as possible. I felt very emotional when I read my letter. I felt vulnerable and small. It was exposing, but I also felt safe. When you have finished, ask your witness to leave. You don't want a post-mortem about what you've just said. You don't want opinions or thoughts. You just need to be heard.

You may feel you want to shake, stomp, move, sing – anything that releases the energy flowing through your body. After you have done this, finish the process with something nurturing like a bath or a gentle walk; just be mindful to be on your own for a little while.

I had an enormous sense of wellbeing after this exercise. I went back to my room and lay on my bed and thought about what I had just witnessed (from myself and the others). It felt as though a shift had taken place. That I had been released. You see, I felt abandoned by Dad and Matt, and telling myself, 'Don't be stupid, they didn't abandon you, it wasn't even their fault. That's really selfish of you to think that, Jill,' was no way to process that feeling. Berating myself meant I was ignoring the feeling, telling myself it was nonsense and then getting angry when it kept returning and reappearing in different parts of my life.

So if the adult part of me knew my dad's death wasn't his fault and that he didn't 'choose' to leave us in the way he did, why did these thoughts still affect me? Because my rational self was not part of that pain. My grief hit me at my core wounds. Four-year-old me did feel abandoned. I didn't understand where he had gone or why.

And then . . . Jill the forty-one-year-old also felt abandoned when Matt died. I was old and wise enough to know that Matt wouldn't have chosen to leave in the way he did either, but that didn't stop the child part of me feeling that way.

If I give these feelings some thought and some empathy, I can say this: 'Yeah, I can see how the four-year-old Jill felt abandoned. She must have been pretty scared and frightened, especially as no one seemed to be able to explain things to her. Poor her. I can also understand that when Matt died so suddenly it must have felt the same.'

If I allow the child to be able to feel her feelings, I can allow the adult part of me to process hers too. And this is what is so powerful about letter writing and witnessing.

Meditation

I've heard so many people say that when they attempt to meditate, their mind starts to wander off and they think about their day/their problems/their kitchen renovations! Yes, yes to all of that. I do too.

A quick peek into one of my sessions could see me start with the best of intentions. Before I know it I am thinking about

a form I have to fill in from my son's school

or a conversation I've had with a friend that didn't feel good and maybe I need to apologize?

and should I get that new throw for the bed?

and why does my life not look as I thought it would?!!!

That's why I attempt to meditate. It's an opportunity to release myself from the curse of attachment to my thoughts. In any given ten-minute meditation I may only get ten seconds here and there of any sort of feeling of space or peace.

And I'll take that. I'll take that any day of the week because, after Matt's death, the incessant thinking and identification with my thoughts meant that there was less room to feel and reflect and do the work I needed to do to grieve. When we identify with our thoughts, we become entangled and believe that every thought is a truth. In my grief, my thoughts were often self-destructive, with huge feelings of hopelessness. Attaching myself to them and not questioning if they were true or helpful meant I felt as if I was being dragged along by them. I was allowing them to be in control.

I think this is why, in the first year of losing Matt, I found meditating came easier to me. I desperately wanted to get quiet and relax my mind and I found complete solace in the silence. The relief of my mind slowing down was so soothing that I was able to sit still for a lot longer than usual. I wasn't distracted by needing to get things done, I was happy to sit and wait and listen. The gift of desperation is a phrase I've learnt in recovery – when we become desperate enough to want to get help. After Matt's death I was desperate enough to want to get quiet. I enjoyed the calm. I needed it!

Meditation has always felt different to me at various stages of my life. I first experienced it at drama school. It was something we did occasionally in our voice classes. We would lie on our mats on the floor in the church hall and be asked to concentrate on the breath. Just listening to the in-breath and then the out. Sometimes we would be asked to visualize colours but mainly it was to try to get us to the place of feeling centred. Which means a place where you have landed fully in your body. Feeling embodied is crucial for an actor; the nerves and anxiety of a first night can feel like physical terror, which is how I also experienced grief. Maybe that's why I was drawn to the industry, because that feeling didn't seem unfamiliar to me. The terror of Dad vanishing from my life. When I perform it's important to be in complete control of my body and my voice. I found early on that the best way for me to do this is through a practice of meditation and breathing exercises, which allow me to calm down my nervous system and to own my body.

In the early days of my grief after losing Matt, when I had multiple moments of anxiety and panic, the thing that helped me most was focusing on my breath. As simple as thinking about the breath going in and going out again. It afforded me the time to realize that nothing bad was happening in that very moment. It gave me a few seconds to bring my heartbeat back to a place where I didn't feel panicked or too overwhelmed. It stopped me from freaking out on the Tube or in a parents' meeting. When I found myself in a state of overwhelm, like I might not be able to control myself, I used to find it helpful to say this to myself:

'You're feeling out of control, Jill. You feel as though you're going to burst into tears and you are panicking. It's OK. You can do that. Nothing bad will happen if you do, but why not try three deep breaths first and then come back to me.'

What this did for me was give myself permission to do the thing that I was most scared of, which was to lose control in a space where I didn't feel it would be acceptable. And then it gave me an option to take myself out of overwhelm. I always found this really helpful because in any given moment of high anxiety what makes it worse is the idea that if I lose control it will be catastrophic. So I gave myself permission to do so, but I also gave myself an option to breathe first and to take stock.

Meditation practice helps us with this. The more we practise the more we can access the moments of calmness when we most need them. Don't think that the only benefit will be during your allocated meditating time. Think of it like a stretching exercise. If you wanted to be able to touch your toes, you would practise stretching each morning. Every day you would do the same exercise and there would be a gradual, incremental progress. Meditation is the same. The benefits accumulate over time, so when the feelings begin to overwhelm, you can remember how to get back to the breath, how you felt in your practice, and ask to go back there.

The challenge with meditation is that progress isn't always obvious, which is why we have to stay aware and why it can feel slow. It's a 'practice', which means the more you do it, the more you will get out of it. But it isn't always linear, it doesn't just take an upward trajectory journey. This for me is the most frustrating aspect! We are always looking for something tangible, something to prove that we are developing, but meditation reveals itself in more subtle ways than that. So, if you practise and stay aware of yourself you will begin to see a different you. Someone who can behave differently if they so choose. Someone who can notice something stirring up inside themselves and decide how they are going to behave, rather than being swept along by reactiveness only to regret it later. It allows us to respond rather than react. As I said . . . transformative.

As my life got busy again after Matt's death, so did my mind, but I still attempt to do it for ten minutes each morning. I've found it's useful to see it as a little gift to yourself rather than a chore. In the way you would sit down with a cup of tea, sit down with yourself.

Find a spot where you won't be disturbed. Somewhere comfortable. Silence your phone and set a timer for ten minutes.

Sit with yourself and try to focus on your breath.

Ten minutes a day is not going to make you feel great immediately, but meditation is cumulative and ten minutes a day over a year may well feel transformative. You will find your own rhythm and your own preferred time of day, but mine is first thing. The most important thing is you do it and you don't judge. Just allow yourself the time and space to be still and focus on the breath.

If you'd prefer to do a guided meditation, there are thousands of free sessions on YouTube. If you don't enjoy the words, the voice, the music, choose another one the next day! Don't allow your discomfort or frustration to be an excuse.

Groups

In the first years after losing Matt, I reached out to a charity called Grief Encounter that works specifically with children and adults who have lost partners or parents. I wanted Harvey to have an outlet for his pain and I thought it would be a good idea if he could make friends with other kids in the same situation. He had been finding it very difficult to sleep and I knew it would be impacting his school life. It was impacting me too. I would worry about him getting up in the night and I would find it distressing when he was upset or scared. I felt like I was failing. He told me one day he felt really angry, he said he wanted to smash some things! So off I went to a charity shop and bought all the ceramics and china they had. I gave Harvey some goggles and a hammer and I let him let rip in our back yard (supervised by me of course). He loved it, he said it felt great and I'll admit that I did a few plates myself!!! Even so, I felt being around other kids in similar positions might be what he needed most.

Grief Encounter would meet up at their building in north London and after a quick chat and cup of tea the kids and adults would separate. The adults would be given an opportunity to talk and share about anything that was on our minds while the kids played together and were encouraged to talk in any way they felt comfortable.

I met some lovely people there and I ended up getting a lot more out of it than I thought I would. Watching Harvey connect with other children in similar situations felt very re-assuring. I could see that he was going to be OK again. We had some great trips away, including a weekend at an Outward Bound facility just outside London where Harvey was able to participate in all the fun activities and the adults could spend time with each other. On the last evening we sat around a fire while we made candles and released balloons for our loved ones.

It's a strange feeling to be among friends that you've known a long time who all have your back but have no idea what you're truly going through. Bereavement made me feel 'different'. At Grief Encounter, we were all in the same boat and we shared a shorthand. We didn't have to try to explain, we knew, and there was a comfort in that.

One lady told me she had to keep busy, filling up every weekend with things to do with her girls because the idea of an empty weekend filled her with dread. I understood that feeling. The structure helps you feel safe and distracts you. I can vividly remember hurtling towards a weekend and wondering how I was gonna get through it without any plans. It was daunting. Another lady had lost her partner and had a son Harvey's age. We talked about how difficult it was and how we felt hopeless and scared. We both found it hard to see a future where we might love again and be happy. I identified with everyone. Even though we were all coping in different ways, I felt a kinship and a deep empathy for the situation we all found ourselves in.

There are many grief charities out there. I know it can be difficult to be in a state of despair and find the courage to call someone you don't know and put yourself in a vulnerable position. I remember feeling almost angry when I contacted them. I was resentful to be in my situation but I desperately wanted to get some help for Harvey. I was scared, really scared, that I wouldn't be able to cope. The idea of being with strangers felt very intimidating. But I also understood the power of being in a room where you all have a shared experience, where you don't feel different or weird and you don't have to explain yourself because everyone has been through it too. It's incredibly powerful. I am so glad we were able to be part of our group. I felt so vulnerable, but they didn't judge me, they simply met me exactly where I was and didn't try to change it.

Often friends and family can't bear to see us in pain. They will go out of their way to try to change the way you feel and they do this because they love us, but it doesn't always feel this way. Sometimes it felt like I was too much. That my sadness was too difficult to be around or to withstand. People can often feel it's their responsibility to make you feel differently. Or your pain mirrors something in them that is unprocessed and they find uncomfortable. In grief, what we often need is to be heard and to feel safe. Not 'fixed' or 'cheered up'. So reach out if you feel able, there are so many of us who want to share with each other and not feel alone.

Rituals

I was first introduced to the idea of rituals on my grief retreat. They can be a powerful way to honour our grief. The ceremony, repetition and conscious preparation can be a very potent way to access our pain. I realize some of you may be slightly put off at the notion of a ritual. It may sound too formal or ceremonial, but we can simply incorporate it into our everyday lives or we can do something a little more intricate. It's all about what feels right for you and what you respond to. I had never done this before and I wasn't quite sure what to expect, but I didn't want to be put off by something just because it felt unfamiliar. I wanted to give it a try to get out of my emotional comfort zone.

It's important to constantly remind ourselves that we need to be attended to while we are grieving. It was often easy for me to get distracted and to allow my responsibilities to take over. It was easier to do that actually. The chores and obligations were things I felt comfortable with, an easy escape route. But caring for your needs will provide benefits that far outweigh the discomfort of feeling like you're in unfamiliar territory.

Taking a bath

The day I came back from the hospital after Matt was pronounced dead is a bit of a blur. I had stayed there the night before with my mam and unsurprisingly had the most fitful sleep I've ever had. I barely slept and when I did I woke up crying or shaking. I arrived home and I remember my mam, my sister Nicola and Polly being in the flat. I was in shock and struggling to believe what had happened. Being back in the place where I had last seen him was disturbing. I can recall being given a cup of tea and some soup and then I remember Polly and Nicola running a bath for me. They said I would feel better. They helped me undress and held my hand as I stepped into the bath. I remember feeling small and vulnerable, and how gentle and caring they were. They left me to bathe, and as I look back on it now, I can see that it was a symbolic act of care. They did it completely instinctively because they loved me, but bathing after a traumatic event is more than just practical. On the grief retreat, often after a particularly intense session we would be invited to go back to our rooms and shower. We would be given time to cleanse ourselves so that we could begin the next session without an emotional hangover.

It was a way to honour what we had just experienced and to let our bodies know that we would be moving forward. Not to forget or get rid in any way, but merely to symbolize what we had unearthed and what may not be useful to us any more. I always took the suggestions we were given even if I didn't feel inclined to do it and over the course of the week I found it to be really useful. I took the time in the water to reflect on the session. I enjoyed letting go of unhelpful ideas as the water ran down my body. I enjoyed taking care of myself when it had been a particularly vulnerable session. It felt as though my grief was being looked after and I was being given the chance to let go of anything surplus that was weighing me down.

Cleansing and washing feature heavily in many rituals because they are a representation of renewal.

I wanted to take this idea home with me from the retreat. To make it ritualistic rather than just something I do on auto pilot. I try to be completely present and do it in a way that feels almost meditative. Focusing on the task and nothing else. Taking time to choose the oils or salts I use, the music I listen to or the candle I want to light. Sometimes I listen to a book or sometimes I choose silence. All that matters is that you're making decisions based on what you need. If you are able, you could ask whoever else is in the house not to disturb you. We just need time to settle and recalibrate, which is impossible to do if we are being shouted for as we bathe!

Taking time and care so that what can normally feel perfunctory can feel considered. The way we clean ourselves can feel completely different if we take care of our bodies the way we would a small baby.

Remember how disconnected to ourselves we can feel when grieving. We can talk to our loved ones, talk to ourselves, perhaps say a mantra as we clean. Always remembering to be present and attentive.

The same can be done in the shower. I would find myself showering a lot after Matt died. If I'd had a particularly gruelling point in the day, I would find the ritual of showering and washing very therapeutic. It gave me a chance to begin my day again whatever time it was.

The retreat gave me this gift. It's such a simple tool and an easy but effective way to incorporate ritual into our daily routines. It's something you could try that converts an action we would be performing anyway into time in our day for reflection.

Creating an altar

Another experience on my grief retreat involved creating an altar. It was something I had never done or thought of before and I was a little wary.

We were all asked to bring along photographs of our lost loves and something small that belonged to them or reminded us of them. On the evening it took place we were led into a barn outside and were greeted with an beautiful altar. My only experience at that point with altars was in my Catholic church as a child. They felt sterile and unwelcoming.

This new way of constructing an altar felt vibrant and so very inviting. It was filled with flowers and foliage and on it were all the pictures of our loved ones. There were trinket boxes and jewellery and lots of other personal items.

I had brought along Matt's orange Matchbox car from when he was a child. He had told me it was his favourite and I loved the idea that he had held it and played with it for hours and hours. There it was among all of the flowers and photographs. I found it incredibly moving.

We all gathered round and took time to look at all the photographs. It was very touching so see the people we had been talking about throughout the week in the pictures. I was moved to see them all arranged together as they were. We gathered round in a group and we were taught a very simple chant. There was an incredible drummer who guided us through what I think was about an hour but to be honest I lost track of time. The simple act of repetition and mourning and singing for all our losses was profoundly meaningful to me. I suddenly understood all those scenes I had seen on the news as a child. People chanting and singing and kneeling and weeping at an altar. It was so cathartic and I slept deeply and soundly that evening.

If this all sounds too out of your comfort zone or too inaccessible for you, then let me suggest a very simple way to perform something like this for you or for a few close friends.

Choose a space in your house or anywhere you feel safe. It can be in- or outdoors, it's completely your preference. Collect some special photographs and mementos of your loved ones. Pick or buy some flowers or whatever it is that you feel is beautiful and lay them down in among your chosen memories. Light a few candles and make sure you are comfortable. If you are alone and you wish to, then you could chant or sing or listen to some music that connects you to your chosen people. The altar is a focal point, it gives us the anchor, the reason to be there. The songs or chants are simply an expression, an outpouring. I have a song that has been in my life for a long time. It's by Nick Cave and the Bad Seeds and it's called 'Into My Arms'. I first walked down the aisle to it, but it's taken on a different meaning for me now. When I listen to it, it moves me deeply and it helps take me to my loved ones. Other times, I want to listen to something that makes me happy and uplifted. The music/singing/chants are all yours to choose. No rights or wrongs.

The hardest thing for many of us is the notion of doing this deliberately. It makes people feel uncomfortable and awkward and yet how many times have parties or nights out ended in a similar way without us giving it a single thought. The nights in pubs where everyone gets a little quieter and the guitarist in the corner begins to play a little softly. People sing together, eyes closed, all of us individually thinking of love and loss and hopes and dreams and disappointments. We don't bat an eyelid then because we feel it has happened organically, that we have been taken by the mood of the night (and the alcohol!).

My suggestion is that you can be your own orchestrator. You can lead yourself into these moments without other people around. Create your own gathering, invite all the people who you've loved and lost to come along. Aunts and uncles, friends and colleagues. Create a pub full of love for yourself and be sure to make yourself as welcome as you've made others. You don't need a night out or any other excuse to simply close your eyes and honour your losses. The ceremony and the preparation of a ritual are there to help us get into a mind frame. To represent a place or focal point for our losses. It's so very personal, and however you choose to do it, I wish you a very special time.

Sea dipping

Cold water immersion has become very popular these last few years. I've been lucky enough to enjoy the benefits and make friends through different dipping communities I have found on social media. The first time I did it I was quite nervous. It was 2021 and I'd been invited by a group of lovely ladies to join them in their morning dip. I wasn't sure I would be able to withstand the cold but I was advised to breathe and try to stay as calm as possible. In I went and as the cold hit me I felt as though I wouldn't be able to stay for any more than thirty seconds. But then something happened. The temperature of the water and the adjustments my body had to make to attune to the cold meant I experienced a pause, a gap. The only thing I could do was focus on my breath and being in the water. It felt peaceful, calm. The cold water, like my grief, can feel as if it's going to overpower me but when I breathe alongside it, when I don't run from it, time slows down and I feel soothed.

When it's time to get out (I usually only manage a few minutes) my body is fully awake and alive. The feeling it leaves me with is a natural high and it can stay with me for the rest of the day. I think there is something about me not wanting to do it that makes me do it! I enjoy overcoming my own discomfort and reluctances. It makes me feel as though I can face my grief more easily.

There is an interesting battle when you dip. Your mind tells you it's too cold and that you can't withstand it, but if you just allow the water to immerse you then you'll find you absolutely can and, when you do, there is very little else you can think about. Your body becomes completely engulfed in the feeling of the cold water and your thoughts slow right down. Once I'm done, I feel as though I've accomplished something. I've overcome a discomfort. The voice inside me says, 'Well, there you go, you've done something that you didn't want to do and was uncomfortable, so you can face whatever else is thrown at you today.' The slowing down and the pause I talked about feel the same as meditation – giving your mind space and letting it know that it doesn't have to attach itself to your thoughts.

Follow the action not the mood

I feel lucky to have been introduced to ways to tackle the confusing barrage of emotions that grief brings with it. I have learnt lessons and been given techniques through AA, personal therapy, the grief retreat and some amazing books, to help me through the storms but, dear reader, I need you to know this: I don't always do them.

I forget, de-prioritize, ignore and reject my grief when it suits me but, luckily, I have another little voice. The helpful, loving one. It has compassion and understands that I don't always get it right, so it can gently nudge me and say, 'C'mon, Jill, I think you need to slow down and take that walk now.' Or, 'I know you don't feel like it but I think an hour in the gym would help change your mindset today and get some energy flowing through you.'

The interesting thing I've noticed is that the more grief work I do the kinder the voice is. The harsh, critical voice that drove so much of my childhood doesn't live rent free in my head any more. It's challenged and questioned and interrogated because I don't want to give it space to grow. The more I process my pain the more I can extinguish the saboteur in my mind. So when you're feeling as if you're not making any progress and there is absolutely NOTHING you feel like doing, just ask yourself this:

Am I waiting to WANT to do this?
Am I expecting to wake up one day and feel enthusiastic
  about processing my grief?

When I answer these questions, it becomes really clear to me what I have to do. Often what I *need* to do to feel a little better is not what I *want* to do. So that's when I try to . . .

Follow the action not the mood

This is a tricky one because I've been telling you this whole time to listen to yourself and connect with your intuition, so you may find this a big old contradiction, but please bear with me.

Don't wait until you feel inclined to exercise or meditate or journal. Do them anyway and commit to at least a few weeks. Then and only then, you can ask yourself if you are feeling any sort of benefit. When Polly first suggested I go to the grief retreat I remember thinking, 'You go on a bloody grief retreat! You go and spend your money to sit with strangers for a week and tell them why you feel so terrible, see how you like it!' The problem was, I knew it was a good idea! I didn't want to do it but I knew I needed to at least try. On the day I left home to make my way there, I was still reluctant within myself. I hated that my life had come to this but again I could sense it was going to be helpful. I put my head into my future self and imagined how it might feel when I left. The two diary entries below show you exactly where I was before and after.

3 April 2017
 Dear Matt, sat in a cafe in Gillingham station waiting for a cab to take me to a grief retreat.
 WHAT THE FUCK
 Who am I? I just don't recognize myself or my life at all.

My face . . . not mine

My feelings . . . not mine

My reality . . . not mine

My narrative . . . not mine

Being a stranger in your own life is the single most terrifying experience in the whole world. The man and woman next to me are talking 'business'.

Matt, I can't tell you how much I want to scream every time I realize you're not coming back. Just give me a goddamn sign. Just show me you're here. I'm desperate. I'm unhappy. Will I ever feel happiness again. Will I stop feeling like a stranger in my own life. A tourist visiting another planet. It hurts so much. My body, my head, my arms, my legs. They all ache with pain. My body is depressed. Totally DEPLETED.

I'm lost, my love. You and Dad have left me. You deserted me when I allowed myself to love and need you totally. You would always say that I didn't allow my vulnerability to show through. Well, how about now, eh? Enough for you? People either ignore me or look at me with such pity and sympathy. They're both unbearable.

8 April 2017

Hey darling, I'm back from the Bridge retreat. Wow! What a wonderful healing time I've had. I know you were with me every step of the way and I know Dad and little Jill were with me too. It was so great to connect with Dad and hear his voice. He kept stroking my hair and making sure I was OK. I loved being with him. Little Jill is so sweet. She's such a sunny, vulnerable little girl and she adores her daddy. It felt like I'd come home, having you, Dad and little Jill with me. We all went for a walk together a few times. It felt so nourishing to have you all so alive inside me. You have changed me, my darling. None of this would be happening without you.

God, Matt, I would have loved you to go on the Bridge. Stuff all the business books, they never dealt with the feelings did they! Thank you for letting me have this experience. I met Emma too. She lost poor Dan. Will you look after him for Emma?

Jill x

Working at processing grief is tough and the inclination is to want to curl up in a ball and shut out the world. Some days this may work but all of the things I have tried, like exercise, writing, sharing, really do help me. You might scream 'I don't wanna exercise!' or 'I hate writing my morning pages!' – this has happened to me a lot. So I don't go to the gym or I throw my book across the room and swear I never want to write another word, but I rarely feel the benefit of that. Over time, I have worked on following the action and ignoring what is more often my brain's way of not wanting to face the day. I've helped to rewire my brain into more helpful choices. I rarely even ask myself the question of whether I'm going to the gym, it's ingrained in me now as something I KNOW makes me feel better. I'm less successful with meditation. I know I feel the benefit but it's not yet become something I do without any conversation in my head first.

If there is something you try and you feel you have given it a fair amount of time and there is no benefit, then tweak it or change tack completely. People swear by running and the benefits it brings to them. Long distance, short distance, I hate it! My knees and hips hate it! And I don't get any kind of euphoria that others talk about. This was a bugbear for me. All through my twenties and thirties I used to think I had to run at least one marathon in my lifetime and then after Matt died and I started to take real notice about how my body felt, one day I thought: *Why? Why do I have to do a marathon? I don't want to. I don't like running.* Now when I see people completing marathons or they tell me they have run twenty miles at the weekend, I don't think, *Oh, I should be able to do that*; I think, *Good on them, that's awesome.* This is all about getting to know ourselves. Yes, get out of your comfort zone, but you have to do what brings you joy. Do what you know will feel good when you look at your future self.

And just because you don't initially enjoy something doesn't mean it's not worth doing. My moods could vary pretty dramatically throughout the day, and if I always waited to feel like doing something before I did it I wouldn't have got out of bed most days.

Grieving is work, processing is tiring, reflecting can be painful. If we stay aware of this we have more of a chance to call ourselves out. We get an opportunity to ask ourselves, 'What am I so afraid of? What is it I am trying to avoid?'

Grief frightened me. It also gave me incredible courage. The fact I was allowing myself to feel the loneliness and abandonment meant that when I was faced with another challenge, for example the grief retreat, there was a voice inside that said, 'Nothing could feel as bad as this. Whatever courage I have to muster to get myself to do this, it cannot be as painful as this!' And I was right.

The grief work may feel challenging and taxing, but the idea of being stuck again (as I was as a child) was way more frightening. The more you do the better you will feel. The more you commit to it the lighter the coat will become. The more you face it the more the grief beach will begin to clear and make way for new experiences. The processing is like a clearing out. You know when you begin a huge sort-out in your house and for what feels like for ever the house looks worse. There's bin liners everywhere, stuff to take to the tip, stuff to give away, stuff that you can't decide whether you want to keep, and you lose all motivation and wish you'd never begun! Then, ever so slowly, you can see it clearing. And then one day when you open a cupboard you can breathe because you can see everything. You might not like everything you see, but at least you can see it. So the work helps me feel more settled, more able to take on new things. When the mess is still there my head can't concentrate, it's too congested.

If it helps, you can also think of it as a physical injury. If we broke our leg and did nothing at all to rehabilitate, it would eventually heal but it may be weaker and less resilient in the future. If, however, we did physio after and learnt how best to regain strength, then we might come out with an even stronger leg or, maybe more importantly, a better understanding of our body. I want to reiterate that the work pays off, it really does.

It can feel counter-intuitive to think the more I cry and the more I process the grief the better I will feel. But it's true, because tears are a symbol of compassion and the more compassion I have the less space there is for criticism. When I hold my pain down and suppress it, it's tiring and it hardens me. I feel brittle. When I give myself space to feel my loss, it's as if I'm being emptied out a little and then I feel I am more capable of having compassion for others. When I was young I hated the term 'Daddy's girl'. If I thought anyone relied on their dad to bail them out, I would roll my eyes and think 'pathetic'. I remember once being told by a colleague that her dad used to get out of bed every morning so he could start the engine running in her car to make it warm for her when she drove to work. Now, as much as I think we should all be independent by that age, I feel pretty sure that my visceral reaction to that 'Daddy's girl' was in large part because I didn't grieve my dad in a healthy way. I was jealous. I couldn't fathom that kind of 'being looked after'. It felt spoilt and entitled. Whether I think it's necessary or not is a completely different thing, but what I know is that now my reaction would be more like, 'Seems a little over the top, but how lovely to have someone care for you in that way.'

After Matt's death I was frightened that I would harden and become bitter, but bitterness is so painful. It's so hard to carry, and I wanted more for myself. I chose me, and with that came humility and a softening towards myself and others. I can hear grief differently now. I've let myself off the hook and I've allowed myself to accept that I've been through some pretty shitty stuff. I try to be less of a taskmaster to myself and more of a cheerleader. I'm a work in progress as far as that's concerned! We don't have to be a reluctant passenger in our grief. We can be a co-pilot and journey through it as opposed to being dragged. Grief work is our friend.

PART 3
A REIMAGINING

Chapter 15

Empty chairs

————

As I write this, I wonder when was the first time I laid the table for dinner and didn't think about the fact there were only two settings or I signed off a card 'Love, Jill and Harvey' without a second thought.

I was at home one evening with Harvey after Matt died. I was making dinner for us both. Our living area was open plan so I could chat to him while I was cooking. As I put the dinner on the table, I suddenly became aware that it was just the two of us. Everything came into hyper focus in that moment. The empty chair, the two knives, the two forks, two glasses. We sat opposite each other and I had to look my little boy in the eyes and watch him cope with my face all crumpled up and wet with tears. There was nowhere to hide and no one to take over and help me out. I had no other choice but to be honest. I wasn't going to lie to him or make up some excuse. I had promised myself I would be honest.

I explained that he hadn't done anything wrong, that I loved the fact that we were together at our table but that it felt like a stark reminder that Matt was gone when we sat down and there was an empty chair. We chatted about him, shared some memories, ate our food and continued with our night. I didn't tell myself that it would never happen again, I didn't berate myself for crying in front of my son, I told myself that it WOULD likely happen again and I should have compassion for myself.

Our loss is always with us. Whether it's at the forefront of our minds, kicking and screaming, or tucked away somewhere during a busy day, the one thing you can rely on is that it will catch you off guard. It will come to visit when you least expect it. My whole philosophy on dealing with grief is to welcome it in and to give it space and attention, but it still manages to catch me off guard and totally overwhelm me.

Mealtimes have been a real trigger point for me. That evening with Harvey it caught me off guard because we had enjoyed many mealtimes just the two of us. His Dad and I separated when he was one so I'd had way more mealtimes with just Harv and me then I ever had with Matt and Harvey. But I knew what our meals together had symbolized for me. I looked forward to cooking and sitting down together. I relished the chat and the silliness at the table. I loved to hear Harvey tell Matt about his day and vice versa. It was the first time since my divorce that I felt I had my own family and then it was gone in an instant, and it was back to being the two of us again.

It made me feel the weight of parenting alone, the knowing that if you're having an off day you can't rely on your partner to take the lead. I was back in the driving seat without a co-pilot. That realization hit me like a truck, and that's why I say we must honour all our losses to fully heal, and what I mean by that is: don't hide in those moments; be honest, be open. There's nothing to be ashamed of. Don't judge it for being too small or insignificant.

I hadn't just lost Matt. I had lost my family unit, my dreams of bringing up my son with a man I loved. The possibility of extending our family and all the things that families do together. It was back to Harvey and I, and me having to be the driver and organizer and instigator. The mam and the dad. Until I was able to accept that was how I felt and admit to all of those losses, I wasn't able to clear the path, to see what else there was to offer and to begin to enjoy the benefits of having that much one-on-one time with my son again.

Another 'empty chair' moment was the first time I signed a greeting card after Matt's death. It may sound silly but it was excruciating. Suddenly seeing my family go from three names back to two again felt like a sucker punch, and it did for quite some time. I believed that Matt would be with us for ever, so the shift was a shock time and time again for my brain. To not see Matt's name alongside Jill and Harvey felt like I was being robbed every time I would write a card. It was a symbol, a stark reminder he had gone.

These moments will pop up time and time again and it's often occasions we haven't given much thought to. We think about the big events, birthdays, anniversaries, and we prepare beforehand, but it's those moments where we first go to call them and realize we can't, when we hear their favourite programme starting and want to tell them to come and watch, the mail that arrives with their name on. It's all those tiny little moments that can be the ones that knock us down, the ones that derail us because we weren't expecting them, and the only thing you can do is tell yourself it's OK. That it's normal and that of course it's going to be painful and hard. Our life with the people we love is made up of tiny little moments that come and go without much thought, but when they are taken they become the big moments.

If you asked me what I would do now if Matt and Dad walked through the door, I'd tell you I would want to sit down on the sofa and hug them. I'd want to hear their voices again and smell them and feel their warm skin. I'd want to have a cuppa with them and hear all about their day. I just miss them!!! It's really as simple as that. We miss our people and all we want is more time. Loss makes us acutely aware of time, how we can feel we have for ever and then it is ripped away from us. Time with each other is the greatest gift and privilege we have.

As I write this, I wonder when was the first time I laid the table for dinner and didn't think about the fact there were only two settings or I signed off a card 'love Jill and Harvey' without a second thought. I have no idea what the answer is and this is the wild journey we take through our grief. We are completely halted by a moment and then at some point as time moves on the same moment passes by without us even noticing.

Please be comforted by this. If we acknowledge all these moments then we have the best chance of healing. We will *know* we are healing when those moments arise and, instead of feeling as though our heart may shatter, we just think: *I really miss them, I truly wish they were here at this table or watching our favourite show on the sofa, but they're not and for this moment I am OK. I can feel deep sorrow and still be OK. I am more than one thing.*

Chapter 16

How we can heal each other

––––––

Pain, even if unspoken, is passed
down through generations. I was very
aware of my mam's pain around her
son . . . On that day at Colin's grave,
we all had a chance to heal a little.

There are times when you receive a message or gift from someone or they share something with you and it touches you in ways you cannot imagine. It's as if they have reached inside your heart and knew exactly what you needed. I had a few of these experiences over the years and they were undoubtedly healing experiences for me. It's taught me how powerful it is to share that vulnerable, hurt part of ourselves with one another. People respond and it makes us feel less alone.

Lucy: I receive a gift from my friend Lucy just weeks after losing Matt. It feels so right and so thoughtful. It's a beautiful, soft, comforting blanket. She writes in the card to wrap myself up in it and let myself be enveloped by it on the days I just need to be held. It feels so kind and nurturing. She knows loss and she knows before I do what will help me in those days ahead. When I wrap myself up in the blanket I am not only comforted, I am being reminded of my friend and how much she cares for me.

I decided I wanted to pass on the same feeling to any of my friends who were struggling. So now if I have a friend who is in pain then I will send them a blanket with the same sentiment Lucy gave me.

Thank you, Lucy.

When we allow ourselves to be honest about our pain, it can unlock the gates to some very beautiful interactions and gestures.

When someone touches us with their grief, it can inspire us to open up ourselves. We will always be moved by someone who is expressing themselves in a way that touches something in us. We feel seen when someone reveals a part of themselves that moves us in ways we cannot do ourselves. We feel inspired to reach out, to let the person know in some way or other that their unfiltered display of grief has provoked us to share with them. I like to think of this as healing in action. When one person's actions inspire another and hopefully carry on to many others. Like a grief chain effect . . .

Polly: I open the box and it's a beautiful bracelet. It has a gold name plate and a grey rope on either side. She has engraved the word WITH on the back of it and bought the exact same for herself. She explains to me that it is to make sure I know that wherever I am she will always be WITH me. We have both experienced loss in our lives and the loneliness that accompanies it, so WITH feels so comforting. She knew she couldn't do the grieving for me, but she could walk alongside me.

Thank you, Polly.

Fiona: There was a mum at Harvey's school. I had always liked her a lot. We used to talk about fashion and jewellery and I would often be asking her where she got her gorgeous wardrobe from. One day she asked me out for a coffee and she shared with me that she had lost her brother. She then gave me a book of poetry and she had earmarked a favourite poem of hers that had helped her express her grief. There was a letter inside explaining how she had come to find the poem. I was so moved. This was a woman who I really liked but I knew very little about. We talked mainly about frivolous things and we laughed a lot. She invited me into her grief and she shared something very private with me. Something that had helped her and she hoped might help me. I found it very touching. I know it wouldn't have been easy for her to open up as she did, but she was prepared to do that to give me something that was important to her. Words that had touched her heart. Grief feels so wretched that our own vocabulary barely seems worthy when trying to explain how we feel. The poem, by E. E. Cummings, is called 'I Carry Your Heart with Me'.

Thank you, Fiona.

Nicola: My sister sent me a gift a year or so after Matt's death and it took my breath away. She had admitted to me that in the aftermath of losing our dad she had purposely kept some memories to herself. She wanted them to be hers, to feel special. I can totally understand this. She was a little ten-year-old girl who had lost her dad suddenly and she needed to hold on to something for herself. Something no one could take away from her. When we lose, we hold on so tight to the things that make us feel better.

I had been talking to Nicola very openly about losing Dad in the wake of Matt's death. The two felt so much the same in my mind even though they were nearly forty years apart. I had explained how confusing it felt to have a huge void in my life with the loss of my father but to not be able to tether the feelings to memories. I was four and didn't remember much at all. It felt scary, almost fraudulent, and it had made grieving for Dad even harder. She must have thought about our conversation and then sent me the gift when she was ready. The box arrived with a letter. The letter said that she wanted to share some of her memories of Dad with me so that I could get a stronger sense of him, a sensory experience. The box contained:

- Cheese and crackers – this was the last thing Nicola had watched Dad eat before he left for football that day. She finds comfort herself when she eats them because she can picture Dad and she feels closer to him.
- A vinyl record of Neil Sedaka singing 'Laughter in the Rain' – she remembers listening to this in the car on the way to the squash club with him. She said she felt special and loved when he took her to the club to see all his friends.
- Brut aftershave – a smell that takes her straight back to him. She said he always smelt nice!
- A vintage leather handbag – she chose this because the smell of leather reminds her of Dad. His football boots, trainers and sports bag. She loved cleaning his football boots for him and applying the dubbing. It made her so happy because she knew how important the boots were to him.

As I sat at my kitchen table, listening to the Neil Sedaka, drenched in Brut and crunching my way through my cheese and crackers, I felt an overwhelming sense of love and gratitude. My sister had allowed me into her memories, she had listened to me and she had responded to the way I felt. She didn't have to do any of that. She had already been an amazing help to me, but this felt like she had given me something that, until then, was sacred to her and only her. To help me heal, she had shared her memories in order to let me feel closer to Dad – and it worked! And maybe it helped her too. Maybe she understood that allowing me in wasn't going to dilute her bond with Dad; it would only make it stronger because it came from a place of deep love and care and it was done with such genuineness.

Thank you, Nicola.

Mam: I never really felt like I had a sense of who Mam and Dad were as a couple or as parents, but one day Mam came to my flat in London and said she had something for me. She handed me a collection of letters. She explained that they were between my dad and her before they had children and he was away working in Leeds on an apprenticeship. They were so beautiful. Two young people completely in love and excited about their future together. Dad was missing Mam so much and he sounded soppy and loving and all the things you should be when you're young and besotted! It was a complete privilege to read them. To have an insight into them as a couple before we came along and before their time was prematurely ended. I had been allowed into a very private world, a world that until then had been only for Mam. This was her way of helping me to get to know the man we all loved and lost. I felt so honoured she did that. It was truly special.

Thank you, Mam.

Matt: Matt had a treasured childhood possession. It was a

Matchbox blue plastic briefcase, full of cars and lorries and all sorts of fun vehicles. I remember when he first showed them to me it brought back such vivid memories of my childhood. I loved the feel of them; I can remember how fast they would go down our homemade ramps in the street. They were made with metal and they had a weight to them that felt so satisfying. Matt's favourite was called the Dodge Challenger. It was bright orange with a blue roof. It has the words 'Revin Rebel' on either side of the doors. One day, he told me he would like Harvey to have them. Harvey was over the moon, he loved them, but as he got older and computers became more appealing they were left at the back of the shelves. Five years after Matt died and now in a new home, I would see this blue case looking all dusty and sad in the storage cupboard. One day I decided I would give it to a charity shop. I wanted another child to enjoy them as much as Matt and Harvey had.

There must have been a tiny part of me that was reluctant to let them go as they stayed in my car boot for a week or so. I had been feeling pretty low and my sister Paula had very kindly booked me a massage; a lady she knew was coming over to her house to give us our treatments. I remember feeling pretty raw. I don't know why specifically, I just remember feeling vulnerable. I needn't have worried. The masseuse was friendly and funny. She immediately made me feel relaxed as she began to chat about her little boy.

'What does he like to do?' I asked.

'D'you know what he loves?' she said. 'Those little cars. He plays with them for hours and hours.'

It's at times like this that you know your loved one is with you and everything feels right. I smiled at her. 'I have a case in my car, full of Matchbox cars, d'you think he would like them?'

'Oh my god, yes,' she said.

The next day I was sent a picture of her son sat on the floor playing with the cars, enjoying being in his own little world. Just as I imagine Matt would have done. I can't tell you what joy it brought me. The timing, the situation, it all felt right. A small bit of reimagining and healing right there in that moment.

Thank you, Matt.

(Oh, by the way, I kept Revin Rebel. He lives on my chest of drawers and always makes me smile.)

It's not only physical gifts that can help repair. Telling our stories and allowing others in can create chains and support of comfort. Even if we aren't talking about our losses, people can still pick up on it. Our energy tells people way more than we'd like to believe. In fact, the less we say the more your closest loved ones will carry a burden for you that even they don't know they are carrying. The unsaid or the unprocessed is very heavy indeed because it carries a mystery and a fear around it that the truth cannot. The truth, although painful, is often easier to bear because we are not carrying the extra weight of a secret wound.

Our grief doesn't have to be the same to be able to share. We tend to naturally gravitate towards people who have had the same experiences as us. This is completely understandable and in the early days of losing Matt I certainly wanted to hear from anyone who had lost partners, especially when the ending was abrupt. I felt it would bring me greater strength and resolve if someone could understand EXACTLY what I'd been through. I did find solace in that, but over time I have found that connecting with another person's grief is way more about the expression of their feelings rather than the exact circumstances of their loss.

Unprocessed grief is passed down through the generations. My mam's offering of the letters was definitely a way to express her feelings about the unprocessed grief around Dad. They made me feel closer to her, like I'd been invited in to her inner world. As we chatted more and more, my mam began to open up about her experience of her stillborn baby. She had talked about it before but I realized she had held a lot of the grief inside and now she was opening up a little more. Mam gave birth to a boy when my eldest sister Nicola was just two. She had a good pregnancy and was unaware there were any problems. Once she started experiencing contractions she went to the hospital. As they examined her she could tell they were concerned; they were not able to hear the baby's heart-beat.

Mam said her labour lasted about seven hours. Her little boy, who they named Colin, was born dead. They took him away immediately. She wasn't allowed to hold him, she didn't even get to see him. She was told it was best not to. This was 1971, and stillbirth was handled very differently. She would tell the story and end with, 'That's just how things were then.'

I could see the pain, almost stuck in her throat. It felt

completely unresolved and my heart broke for her. Maybe because we were both so cracked open from losing Matt and all it had brought up, we began to chat more about the possibility of getting some kind of closure.

I encouraged her to contact the hospital; I felt sure they would have a record of where his body had gone. She did, and the hospital were very helpful and understanding. They were able to let my mam know in which graveyard her son was buried and in what area. We went along as a family and had a small gravestone made with his name and date of birth engraved on it. We chose a spot in the area we had been directed to, and there among all the other tiny babies who didn't make it we planted his nameplate and cried as we remembered our little brother. Almost forty-four years later my mam was able to give herself a small gift by expressing her pain and allowing it to propel her to reach out to the hospital. All of us, including grandchildren, were there to be part of honouring him, and now my mam has a place to visit, which will hopefully help her grieve her beautiful son who she carried for nine months but was never allowed to meet.

This collective sharing of grief is so powerful. Pain, even if unspoken, is passed down through generations. I was very aware of my mam's pain around her son. She may have only spoken about it sporadically, but the sadness and anger were palpable. On that day at Colin's grave, we all had a chance to heal a little. For the first time, I felt like I had a brother. When Nicola shared her personal memories of Dad with me, it brought us closer and helped alleviate some of the shame she had felt about keeping them to herself. She had believed that in sharing they would lose some of their potency, but it did the opposite because she saw the effect it had on me. Everyone in my family has their own personal story of loss and grief and we all deal with it differently, but these moments let us know that it's safe and it's allowed.

Sometimes grief needs a place to live. It helps us to know there is somewhere we can go where grief is welcome and expected. Which is why we have graveyards, cemeteries, monuments and personalized park benches. It gives us permission.

The need for a place to grieve was perfectly illustrated in a story I read some time ago about the Wind Phone. The Wind Phone is a real place in Iwate Prefecture in north-east Japan. A man called Itaru Sasaki installed a phone box in his garden. It is at the foot of Kujira-yama, just next to the city of Otsuchi, one of the places worst hit by the tsunami on 11 March 2011. Inside the phone box is a disconnected telephone that carries voices into the wind.

Thousands of people make the pilgrimage each year from all over the world. To a disconnected telephone! Sasaki-san explains that the journey to the telephone can be arduous. Multiple trains and no signposts to speak of. He says, 'It's a sort of bridge that connects the world of the living to the world of the dead. Just getting here is an exercise in mindfulness.' He explains that it is intentional that there are no signposts. The act of wandering, losing oneself in the landscape and uncertain when you will get there, means that you will begin to connect and reformulate memories of the person you have lost so that when you arrive at the telephone you are open, fuller and more aware. 'They are ready to create a new relationship with the dead.'

I find this whole idea so moving and profound. If we are to create a new relationship with the dead, then it really can be anything you want. For some it may be the wind telephone, for others it's music or landscapes. There are no rules. The way you connect is up to you.

Recently I heard someone on a podcast explain how after they lost their mother they felt compelled to talk to other women her age. He observed a group of friends having breakfast together and he asked if it would be OK to pay for them. He explained he had lost his mum and watching them together reminded him of her. One lady burst into tears; she had lost her son and he was a similar age to him. This is a beautiful example of someone acting on their grief and sharing an act of kindness that turned out to have a more profound effect than he ever dreamt. It may seem like a bold thing to do, but bravery is often rewarded in beautiful ways. Be brave with your grief. You can express it in so many different ways. Random acts of kindness, opening up when it feels right, but always allowing, allowing, allowing. We get to be in charge of our boundaries, of course, but if we stay open then we could be on the receiving end of some pretty special moments.

I had one of these after a visit to a salon in central London that I went to for years to get my eyebrows threaded. The lady who owned it was lovely and always very intuitive. It had been six months since losing Matt. I didn't say anything to her but I remember feeling pretty heavy and sombre. She must have sensed I was in a bad way and after my eyebrow treatment she offered me a cranial massage. I was touched she wanted to help and I felt extremely emotional. She held my head in her hands and the way she was massaging the back of my neck and my temples felt so soothing. The sensation of my head being held and how secure that made me feel meant I pretty much cried for the whole treatment. It didn't matter; I knew I was safe there.

After finishing my massage she told me about a man who had helped her through some really dark times. I took his number and booked my first session. He was a Buddhist and his approach was different to anything I'd experienced before. I saw him for no more than five sessions, so our time was fleeting, but it made a lasting impression on me. He would chat to me for twenty minutes or so at the beginning of our session. I'd let him know where I was at and what was going on for me that day. We'd then move on to some body work. Sometimes he would get me to walk around the room as we chatted, and he would be observing my physicality and my energy. I would then lie on the massage table and he would work on different parts of my body. As he did this he would talk to me, he would ask where I was and what I could see. My visions were always very clear, almost like a movie, but there was one image in particular that kept returning at each session.

I'm standing on a battlefield. It's desolate and dry. I'm thirsty and I'm alone. My body is battered and bloodied and it is deathly quiet. I am neither scared nor vigilant. There is no sense of the battle beginning again, just a deep knowing that I have to get myself home and that the real work is only just beginning. My body feels as though it has walked thousands of miles but even so it keeps on, always putting one foot in front of the other. I'm not sad, I'm exhausted.

A few weeks later I'm in another session and we are discussing my dad. I'm lamenting the fact that I have very few memories of him and I'm not sure how to access them or indeed if there are any. We chat and do some more body work. I sit on the floor as he talks to me and I have the most vivid recollection of my dad.

I'm one year old. He's sitting on the floor in the living room, his legs in a V shape, and I'm between them. He's holding me around my waist and throwing me up in the air. Each time he throws me he laughs and I squeal with delight. It feels so very real. He is staring up at me as I'm suspended in the air and his whole face is smiling. I burst into tears; it feels amazing.

I have no idea if this was a memory or an imagining and I don't really care. All I know is that I had made enough space in my body and I had stopped fighting for long enough to let love and joy into my heart and, most importantly, my dad.

If we resist it, grief feels like a perpetual battle. The visions I was having of myself on the battlefield were a sign that I needed to return home to myself. It was clear that the war was over and my body needed to surrender to the loss. Once I could fully accept that Matt and Dad were gone, then I could drop the fight inside me. When I eventually left the battlefield I could see and hear more clearly; I could tend to my wounds. And, when I did, I experienced the vision of my dad. It was so happy and pure, but most importantly deeply healing. It connected me to him in a way I'd never experienced before and for that I was truly grateful. I was also grateful to my beautician; she saw something in me that she knew needed attending to. She could have easily ignored this but instead took time out to give me cranial sacral therapy, which helps release emotional blockages, and then she gave me the gift of directing me towards a practitioner who opened up another part of me and was a powerful part of my healing process. Thank you. I will never forget your kindness.

The chain of events that led me to this place will always be a reminder of the power of communal healing. It took so many kind and thoughtful people offering me physical and emotional gifts to get me to a point where I felt I could leave the battlefield of grief.

Chapter 17

A new storybook

———

I watch as the story of each of our lives unfolds and I think about how there will be new chapters, chapters I could never have imagined, chapters that look significantly different to the ones before.

When Dad died, I still had my mam. I was four, so I looked to her to guide and care for me. She was my mam and the only person in the world I felt truly safe with. The idea of what I was going to do next didn't occur to me. I was too young to be able to articulate and understand the loss on a cerebral level, so it was all felt and stored inside of me.

When Matt died, I was not only able to feel the loss, I could understand it too. My mind liked to remind me what had been taken away. Not just a partner and a loving relationship, but a marriage, a baby, a family, a house and future that looked to be all I had ever wished for. Of course we can never know what the future holds for us, but my mind had some very clear ideas and I lost all of those hopes and dreams along with losing Matt.

This is where death, and especially untimely death, can be very difficult to process. We saw a future with our friend/child/sibling/partner. We talked about plans with them. Places we would visit and adventures we would have. Often this part of loss can be just as difficult to accept as losing the person themselves. A whole life seems to die alongside our loved one and with it a whole version of us that we had envisioned so clearly. We can't visualize our future because it doesn't exist any more. The path ahead has been terrorized, destroyed, obliterated.

So what do we do? How do we imagine a future when the

storybook has been torn apart? Were we fooling ourselves that we could write our own story anyway? Or: what if life is about lots of different stories and you have to be prepared to tear one up before you begin another? What if the new story contains happiness, joy even?

Death confronts us with the idea that writing your own story was only ever a fantasy. No one really knows how life will turn out. We are plunged into a world where every page, every sentence, is unfolding in front of us and it all feels very strange and unfamiliar.

You may be screaming at me right now. Telling me that the world makes no sense without your person in it and I should be ashamed to think that a different story could be just as good. Well, I'm not here to tell you that. I'm just wondering if you'd considered it. I hadn't.

In the early days of losing Matt I could not comprehend how a life without him in it could possibly be as good. I had lost him and my dad and I was going to spend the rest of my life wondering where the hell they were and feeling angry and deeply sad. And then I heard about a book called *Option B*. Sheryl Sandberg (COO of Meta Platforms) had co-authored it with Adam Grant (professor, author and organizational psychologist). I wouldn't have normally gravitated towards it because I presumed it would be too corporate and basically tell me to 'pull my boot straps up', but I'd heard Sheryl talk on a podcast about losing her husband, the circumstances of which were very similar to Matt's death. I got curious and was interested to know how she had dealt with the feelings in the aftermath. I honestly didn't know much about the concept at all, so I was reading it blind. What I do remember is feeling a little irked. I was being challenged, it felt uncomfortable, so I got more curious.

Sandberg introduced me to the idea of facing option B without it feeling like I'd been handed a booby prize. Option B is the option you're left with after your loss. Your person has left and so life is going to look and feel different without them in it. You can reject option B because it's not what you want, or you can grab it and interrogate it and give it a damn good try. The idea took hold inside of me. I had experienced the story of my life being ripped apart in front of me twice now. I knew full well that we really don't know what is round the corner. How could I possibly know that option B wouldn't be just as good when I had no idea what was waiting for me?

This doesn't mean for a second that we have to be happy in any way about our circumstances. This is all about acceptance, and we all come to this at different stages. But once we have accepted our situation, we then have a choice as to how we are going to approach the rest.

We have two choices in grief. We can stay in the same book feeling bitter and angry every day that the story doesn't have the ending we wished for, or we can do the bravest thing you will ever do in your life. Pick up a new book, with blank pages, and watch the story unfold in front of us. Feeling at turns terrified and confused, and maybe, just maybe, happy?

Walking a different path can lead us to find riches and treasure that we never knew possible. Accepting that option A has left us can be tough, but what if we saw option B not as subordinate but just different? What if we gave as much vigour and verve to option B as we did to A?

If we do our grief work then my belief is that we can look at our new story and move forward with curiosity, an open heart and maybe even a teeny little bit of excitement. If we don't do our grief work and process our losses then we may find ourselves stuck in a loop and unable to move forward on our new path.

Psychologist Martin Seligman in his book *Learned Optimism* talks so brilliantly about the 3 'P's, which can obstruct our recovery and stop us from pursuing a new story.

- Personalization – the feeling that we are at fault, that somehow the loss could have been avoided if we didn't do x, y or z. This can keep us stuck in a loop of self-blame and shame.
- Pervasiveness – the belief that the event will affect all areas of our life. This feeling we have when it seems as though nothing will ever be right again. That EVERYTHING is ruined.
- Permanence – that the wretchedness will never go away and you will feel like this always.

These are pretty common feelings in loss and they will stop us from seeing a possible new path. They are unhelpful and obstructive.

Once I began to see that a new story may hold inside it a

life beyond my wildest dreams, then I began to open up my heart. The pain didn't leave me, but the possibility of change and opportunity created space for something new, something I hadn't thought possible.

As the years passed by after Matt's death, I gently and slowly began to feel energized again. I started to feel braver. I let go of the idea that I wouldn't find love again. My ambition returned and I was able to talk to my agent about roles I wanted to be considered for. Always safe in the knowledge that I may not get any of these things and I would still be OK. This may not sound like much, but having conversations about the future, and wanting to be challenged again, was a huge relief. It was a respite to feel something other than that I was just surviving.

And then the next new idea in *Option B* was presented to me. Can you thrive after loss? Is it possible to become a more successful, happier and more fulfilled version of yourself? The answer is yes, but that it may not arrive in the way you imagined.

The mere fact that I was reading words like 'thrive' and 'more fulfilled' made me feel less scared. I knew it wasn't a guarantee, but somehow the idea that life wasn't going to be a terrifying case of just getting through made me feel like happiness may not have completely eluded me.

Post-traumatic growth is the positive psychological change that results from a traumatic event or highly challenging life circumstance. I was under no illusion that traumatic events would have a negative impact on my life, but I became more interested in what I could possibly gain from them!

So it's over seven years since Matt died and forty-five for

Dad. Although I have lost so much, I have also gained a huge amount through my journey.

I've found some perspective. When I am feeling incredibly overwhelmed at life (as I am now, actually, as I write this), I can look back to those days when just waking up was a struggle. When I literally felt as though I wanted to crawl out of my own skin because it felt so unbearable and I can think: *Well, at least I'm not there today, and if I got through that then I can get through this.* I can always remember how bad it was and if I compare it to how I feel today then it pales in comparison. This is a gift. A true gift. If you've been to the gates of despair and you have survived then you know you have strength and resilience. I have a new sense of perspective around work; I know I have something of value to offer but I know not everyone will want it. Simple, but pretty powerful in my line of work. This perspective can take me back to feeling calm, it stops the overwhelm and the sense of loss of control.

I have talked about gratitude a lot already but my ability to be grateful has increased tenfold since I worked through my grief, which has allowed me to be less self-piteous. Grateful, because there is always a worse scenario we can think of, but please remember that isn't to say we are not still devastated. It's just a shift away from it feeling very personal and self-pitying to a knowing that we all suffer, that life *is* suffering. The ability I have now to be grateful for the minutiae of life is miraculous. If you told me I could be the type of person who would be really grateful for a flower or a smile from a stranger, I wouldn't have believed you. When you practise gratitude, it becomes stronger. Your appreciation muscles grow! So, when I have a crappy day and I'm feeling low, I find great strength in being able to write down my ten reasons to be grateful – and believe them!

My relationships have improved and changed shape in the aftermath of my grief work. I have some friends now with whom I can cut through all the crap and get straight to the heart of what we want to say to each other. I have a dear friend, Gunilla, who lives in Sweden. We have been through a lot together. She was a beautiful friend to me after I lost Matt. In recent years she has lost her sister and her dad. She has experienced enormous grief and it has changed her as it does all of us. We were always able to talk to each other but now we have a much deeper understanding. It's a fast track to each other's hearts. Our relationship has a profundity to it and we both know we will walk alongside each other until it's time for one of us to leave.

We talk a lot about feeling lucky to be alive, but I'm not sure we fully embody that until we lose someone. When I took time to really think about Matt and Dad's life being cut short, it struck me how lucky I was to still be here. These were two men who lived life fully and with gusto. I owe it to them and to all the others who have tragically been taken too soon to be grateful that I'm still here.

Finding meaning. Birth, death, love, hopes, dreams, achievements. They have all taken on such a deeper meaning for me. When my great-niece Goldie was born recently, I wasn't just thrilled to have a new cute addition to the family. I felt moved by the arrival of new life. I felt excited at the new energy of this soul entering the world. When someone falls in love, I am captivated by their story and the connections they are making. I don't merely see it as a love story any more; I see two souls who have found each other and need to learn something from each other before they move forward.

I watch as the story of each of our lives unfolds and I think about how there will be new chapters, chapters I could never have imagined, chapters that look significantly different to the ones before. And I catch myself when I begin to think I am in control and steering the ship because I know now, this is the great illusion. We are merely passengers! We have no idea what's coming next for us. I've struggled with that thought because I've focused on what the next disaster may be and how to protect myself, but what about the next windfall? I can't avert calamity by thinking pre-emptively. But I can try to live in the present, which means not lamenting the past or worrying about the future. The future I have come to accept is unfolding in the moment.

However . . . a passenger doesn't have to be passive. You can be as involved and as passionate as you choose in your life. This whole book has been an attempt to let you know that grief will happen whether you want it to or not. The only thing we can have a say in is how we deal with and react to it. This is the same for all aspects of our lives. I want the quality of my and your experience in the story to be the best it can be. I don't want to be offered my dream job if I haven't worked on my self-belief. I will doubt myself and take away the joy. Or what a waste it would be to be introduced to someone who is everything I've ever wanted but because of not working through my grief I let them go, scared I'll lose them anyway. We are always being given opportunities in life. Whether we are ready and able to see them as that is up to us. Luck is where opportunity and preparation meet. So prepare to feel as good as you can, stay open and curious to opportunities appearing, but always gently remind yourself that the story will write itself.

Chapter 18

The grief gift

———

Friendships, romantic relationships and even encounters with strangers. I can connect with people and communicate with them in a way I wasn't able to before.

Can grief ever be a gift? Can we ever truly look back and be grateful that we have lost?

I think being grateful for losing can seem like too much of a stretch for most of us, but what I can appreciate is the profound learnings in my loss.

I've learnt that no one ever became more enlightened by getting everything they wanted. A spiritual journey is not about getting what you want, it's about getting what you need. And the journey is not about what happens to us, it's how we respond to what's happened to us.

When we lose, we go on a journey. It is a journey of pain, anger, sorrow, denial and, at some point, if we allow ourselves, deep humility. If we have done our own grief work then it becomes impossible for us to hear of someone else's loss and not feel deeply moved. Our capacity for empathy multiplies because we have an intimate understanding of what someone has gone through and it brings with it a deep respect. This is a huge gift. This gives me a perspective and respect for people. It compels me to send positive thoughts and prayers towards people on the other side of the world. People who I don't know and will never meet but feel connected to. I too, without knowing, will have received another stranger's love.

More joy

I know life is random and terrible things happen every day, but if I am to believe that wholeheartedly then the opposite also has to be true. The world is in a constant state of tension, yin and yang. There can be no good without evil. There will always be wonder and love and joy and pain and terror and heartache. It's how the world works and no one escapes it all. I am learning that if I really want to access joy, if I really want to be able to live a full life with the entire palette of emotions, then I mustn't skip past the feelings that are more difficult. In doing so I rob myself of a fuller life.

The more I accept that, the more joy enters my life.

Through a lot of the therapy work, I have realized that accepting that bad things can and do happen every day hasn't made me a more negative person or more susceptible to bad luck. It's done the opposite, because I can now see that there are a million small things that happen every day that are in themselves little miracles. Things I never used to notice. I can feel grateful for things I previously took for granted. One of my favourite things is being in the car with my son and singing *Hamilton* at the top of our voices. He takes Hamilton, I take Burr. We harmonize, we laugh, we make up the words, and we sing like no one is listening! It's the simplest pleasure but it brings me joy.

I know it may seem hard to believe but, to put it bluntly, the loss has made me more grateful to be alive. I now understand the wonderment of being able to live. I can appreciate my body and the fact that it works. I feel so thankful for my health. I can whinge about the lines on my face and the grey hairs, but also feel so grateful I get to be here another day. Being an actor means you get to see yourself through the eyes of others. When you read the description of your character and it says 'mum of three teenagers, tired and struggling' and my ego goes '*me*, mum of three?', but my next thought is 'hell, yeah, that's how lucky I am.' Some things are easier for me to accept than others, but when I can, I try to shift my focus onto the gratitude for being able to live another day rather than the number of days my loved ones have had taken away from them.

When you experience the dark side of life and allow yourself to walk the painful path to healing, you will find the ability to access joy and happiness so much more potently. To know deep grief is to know deep love. When we allow ourselves to grieve deeply we are allowing ourselves to love deeply.

When I dropped the idea of trying to control my grief, I let in the love that I had been pushing away for years. Lots of different kinds of love.

Friendships, romantic relationships and even encounters with strangers. I can connect with people and communicate with them in a way I wasn't able to before.

I can now forgive myself for all my past wrongs while still holding myself accountable, and I understand absolutely that most of us are just trying to do our best. Sometimes we fall short and other times we exceed expectations but we will all need one another at some point in our lives.

It takes courage to be in pain because pain is scary. Some of us think fear is the opposite of courage. But how can you be courageous if you haven't been fearful in the first place?

I let grief bring me to my knees, I was humbled by it and I eventually began to enjoy life more. Though, it's important for me to add that I don't experience this every day and I certainly find myself falling into old habits and ways of thinking, but I have tools now that help me make choices.

I interrogate my thoughts. Are they real? If I am at work and I'm conjuring up a story about how someone doesn't like me, I ask myself the question, 'Jill, is this really true? Can you know for sure it's true?' That's often all it takes for me to see there is no real evidence for my thoughts. I move my body. I know how important it is for my mental health to move my body in some way or other. I talk to a trusted friend because I've learnt the power of sharing and identifying with others who understand. It makes me feel less alone. Or I connect with nature, I turn my gaze to something that teaches me that change is inevitable and I don't have to be scared of it. All of this I learnt through being in pain. Pain that felt unbearable. Pain that forced me to find a different way through life. I can see very clearly the complexity of our hearts and that we are all on a journey. Every single one of us. I can accept that we all have our pain to bear. That no one escapes it. We all experience loss in some form or other and we WILL lose people we love. That is a fact.

When and how is up to the universe. When you allow your-self to be humbled by the love you felt for the person or life you have lost, when you let it bring you to your knees – when you are open and receptive to what it wants you to receive, it will pick you up and put you back on your feet with a superpower. With something so powerful and simple you won't believe it. It will give you understanding and insight. It will make you feel less alone and more connected.

No one NEEDS their loved one to die to be taught a lesson. That's not what I'm suggesting. But when I listened to the lessons that loss had to teach me, they were lessons I deeply needed. Grief has made me a better person. I have more sympathy, more understanding, weirdly more faith that the universe has my back, more trust in others. I have let go of the idea that I am alone and that everyone I love will abandon me.

This has not come easily and it hasn't been linear. I have rocked, sometimes violently, between these thoughts, but the more I have investigated them and challenged myself, the harder it is for me to believe that I am singled out to suffer. We are all in this together. The bad and the good ripples through us all. I didn't wake up one day and think, *I am not alone and the people I love will not automatically leave.* Rather, through time, learning from others and identifying with them, I have learnt that we are way more similar than we are different. We are all making our way through this life and no one has the secret password!

We ALL struggle, but once we have experienced that darkness we will sense it in those around us and it will change our perspective. It will grace us with humility and gratitude. We will never forget the despair we felt and we will be grateful that we are standing up again.

Grief disconnected me from myself and from the rest of what the world had to offer, and when I made the decision to walk alongside it and let it teach me, it connected me back again. Connection, the thing I so longed for when I was a little girl, came back to me through my grief. Connection was what I needed. To myself, to the world and to others.

This is my gift, and it only came to me because I allowed the sadness to come. And it still does.

Writing this book has meant many days when I've cried and mourned and remembered, but that's all good. I've never felt worse after a cry, only better. It's a release, and the more you release your pain the more you can access real joy and laughter. I don't think I've ever laughed as hard as I have since my journey through loss. When you stop holding on so tightly, life becomes easier to smile at. There are always gifts to be had, everywhere.

You don't have to be happy that you're grieving to receive them, you just have to listen and be patient. They will always reveal themselves.

Life will always challenge us, but if we can ask, 'What is this trying to teach me? What can I possibly learn from this experience?', then we have a better chance of receiving the wisdom that is waiting for us. We reach and grab outwardly when we are scared. I do it all the time. A new jumper, a night out, a holiday. All of these are fine, but what we forget to do is go inward. That's where the gifts are. In the space inside. Don't think of your grief journey as climbing a mountain. Think of it as going down the mountain, going deeper, listening more carefully, getting quieter. All of this will mean that when you're ready you will sing louder, dance harder and laugh longer.

Chapter 19

Signs

———

I look at it and ask if he's OK
about the date. On comes 'Budapest'
and there's my answer.

I took a trip away to Greece in the summer of 2017. It was six months after Matt's death.

It was a small hotel with a private beach. I had chosen it because I wanted to be somewhere that felt secluded and safe. It was beautiful. It felt serene and just what I was after. My plan was to be on my own, to read, to sleep and to enjoy the silence. I had purposely booked it so I would be there for my birthday. I couldn't bear the idea of waking up to a flat without Matt and having to spend time with anyone pretending to enjoy my day. I was turning forty-two and felt as though I'd had my future taken away. The plans, the hopes, the dreams, all gone.

It's the day before my birthday, 14 July. I'm on a bike, exploring the area. It's really hot and the cycle helmet is making me feel hotter. I'm feeling free and I'm enjoying watching the world go by. I stop at a local beach and watch a family play together. I can't help but feel the sting of what is missing. I tell myself that it's OK, that I'm OK and this is a new journey. An unexpected one, but it's all I've got.

I jump back on the bike and spend another couple of hours exploring. I talk to Matt throughout the whole bike ride. Time goes slowly but I'm glad I'm out and by the time I get back to the hotel I feel like it was the right thing to do.

I park the bike up against the tree at the hotel and take off the helmet. As I turn to leave I take one last look at the bike and that's when I realize that printed in white letters along the crossbar is 'MATTS'.

I do a double take. Matts? I'm in Greece, it's a hire bike and it says Matt's! I smile and in that moment I am totally delighted. It feels magic. I send a WhatsApp message to my family and off I go back to my room. Coincidence? Maybe, but I like to think he was there with me for that whole holiday and certainly on the bike ride.

I longed for signs from Matt in those first few months. I couldn't bear the thought that we weren't able to communicate any more so I needed to know he could hear me.

It's 2019. I'm still looking for signs but these days they tend to catch me more off guard. Sometimes I feel a little disillusioned by it all. I doubt anyone is really there and I feel a bit stupid for thinking otherwise. It's two years after Matt's death and I'm about to go into an audition. It's for a part I really want. I wait in the upstairs of an old building just behind Tottenham Court Road. I'm really nervous and I don't have anyone to share the feeling with so I start talking to Matt (in my head). I tell him how I'm feeling and if he can send any good-luck vibes towards me that would be great. A song begins to play in reception. 'Under the Pressure' by a band called the War on Drugs, from the album *Lost in the Dream*. It's not a song you hear being played often at all, certainly almost never on the radio. Matt LOVED his music and he took me to a concert of theirs at

Brixton Academy to promote this very album. We had been dating for two months. We had a great time. We kissed and held each other as we watched the band and I felt nineteen again. I fell in love with him that night. Hearing the song reminded me how real that love felt. The way he looked at me and told me he'd 'won the jackpot' when he met me. I felt like he was with me, cheering me on. I walked into my audition feeling amazing and, guess what?

I didn't get the job! Turns out he's not that powerful!

I still long for signs today, but as my life becomes busy that part of me becomes closed off and I have to make a conscious effort to stay connected and be in communication with my loved ones and with the world itself. This often happens when I'm feeling emotional or scared. I remember that I have to ask questions, be quiet and wait and listen.

It's May 2023. I've been living back in the North-East now for a couple of years. The pandemic hit, the world slowed down and I found myself being pulled back home, or more specifically to the sea. Harvey and I have a new home and we can watch the waves crashing against the pier from our living room window. He has been at his new school for over two years now. I worried he might struggle with the transition but he's managed beautifully.

It was a difficult decision to leave. I had been in London since I was eighteen years old and I thought I'd be there for ever. Apart from the obvious pull of being closer to family and friends, I found myself searching for a new way of living.

London had given me so much, but something was bringing me closer to the water. I feel relaxed here, soothed. It's difficult to describe other than to say it feels right. I miss my friends down south. Leaving Polly was a wrench, but even though I knew I would struggle, something was telling me that I had to stretch myself. I had to be brave and follow my instincts. My head was hesitant but my heart was louder and it guided me.

It's over six years since I lost Matt and I'm sat on the floor outside my bedroom listening to the radio, doing my make-up. I'm getting ready for my first official date with a new man. I'm chatting to Matt, telling him that I'm nervous, that this man seems different and I've a feeling it might go somewhere. Matt was in a male choir and one of the songs they performed was 'Budapest' by George Ezra. He said he loved singing it because it reminded him of me. Since he died, the song has followed me everywhere. There is a picture beside my leg of the two of us in New York. It's in a black frame and I love it. I look at it and ask if he's OK about the date. On comes 'Budapest' and there's my answer.

A few months later I'm arriving for a BBQ at 'new man's' house. We've been together for three months now. As I walk into the garden he gives me a huge smile and on comes the song. 'New man' has no idea about the significance, he looks so happy to see me, and in that moment I feel as though I'm exactly where I'm supposed to be.

When we grieve, we desperately ask for signs from our loved ones, something to know they can see us, they are proud of us or they are with us. The more we keep an open heart, the more receptive we are to the signs around us. At least that has been my experience. And the interesting thing is, no sooner do they come than I am batting them away, shrugging them off as a coincidence or something daft. Why do I do that? Why do I ask for communication and then, when it is given to me, tell myself I am being silly? It's what happens to me when I'm feeling disconnected: I lose any sense of an energy between myself and my loved ones and I start to feel isolated and hopeless. The magic of the world leaves me and things become stupid or trite. I am usually in fear in these moments. Feeling stuck and anxious. It's a sign that I haven't been doing any of the things that I know help me get back to me. I want to live in the world of signs and magical moments; it makes life more beautiful. They're precious and it upsets me when my head sometimes rejects them. I know these things can never be proven and there will be many of you who don't believe, but I'm interested in the psychology of why we can't always keep hold of the beautiful feelings that the signs give us.

When I feel really stuck and frightened, I find myself thinking, *Well, if they can see and hear us, why are they allowing all this bad stuff to happen? Why aren't they intervening?* I am putting them in some crazy position of power as my protector, but that's not what they ever were anyway!

Yes, Matt and Dad looked after me, but they couldn't stop bad things happening or manipulate situations in my life, and it's a mistake for me to think they can do that now. So Matt turning up to wish me good luck in my audition is enough. I ruin it for myself when I think: *It can't have been him because I didn't get it!* Just writing this is making me cringe. Why would I expect so much of my loved ones? They are not my higher power, nor should they be. I want to start taking the signs, however small, for what they are. That way I think I can keep hold of them and not brush them off when things don't work out.

I think this goes back to my deepest fear of feeling un-lovable. The abandonment that goes way back to when I was four. The rejection of the signs is as much a rejection of myself as it is of the moment. 'Don't be stupid, they're not looking after you or thinking about you, Jill, you're on your own, kid, always were, always will be.' I feel sad for this part of me. She's also quite destructive. She wants to tell me there is no point to anything or anyone. She's a nihilist. But it doesn't feel like me when I'm there. It only feels like a slice of me, and the only reason she doesn't want me to experience joy is because she's afraid it will be taken away from her again. So she would rather not feel it in the first place.

That's why I try to stay open and connected. It's easy for me to shut down, but it hurts there, it's lonely and I want to heal that part of me rather than letting it rule me. I want to stay open to signs and the connection they bring as much as I can. It feels like a much more hopeful place to be in.

Chapter 20

Learning to love and be loved again

———

I can allow myself to be happy and in love without feeling any guilt. I can be vulnerable and scared and understand where it's coming from. I can be free and open, allowing myself to be seen without fear of abandonment.

No matter what relationship we have to our lost loved one, it can feel very difficult to walk through the waters of love in grief. There are people in our life who love us very much, and want to continue to love us, but it can be a challenge. Similarly, there are people in our lives who are used to receiving love from us and we may not have it to give in the way we once did. Not for a while at least.

Grief changed my energy. Things I once enjoyed faded for a while, things I laughed at no longer raised a smile. I did regain the things I wanted back in my life, but some just didn't feel like they fit any more.

For the people around me I sense it may have been tricky. They had to get to know a new version of me, and it may have scared or even angered them when they couldn't find the part of me that felt so safe and familiar to them. That's why we ask for time and patience. We ask those around us to let us heal without constraint because in those early months it feels as if EVERYTHING reminds us of our loss. As if no place is a safe space because the grief is ever present. This must be hard for our partners, children, friends and family. They are dealing with new reactions in us every day and that's why I have spoken about how important those around us are.

My feeling is if you can be as honest as possible to your loved ones, then you have the best chance of reimagining your relationships with this new version of yourself. They can only be as flexible as your honesty. We can't keep it all to ourselves and expect them to understand the grief at every moment.

Conversely, they have to understand that sometimes we don't have the capacity to explain what is going on and what we need is space and patience. It is very much a journey for all those around us.

After I lost my dad I had to learn how to let myself be loved without controlling the outcomes. I needed to learn that I could survive a partner leaving me, a relationship breaking up or a friendship breaking down without it taking me under. My first big relationship heartbreak felt so bad but I knew it had to happen. After my divorce and a couple of years into my sobriety, I really thought I had nailed it! *Yes*, I thought. *I can deal with severe loss and disappointment, I am strong enough to go through these experiences and know that I can withstand them.* It gave me courage and it affirmed what I always knew: that I have resilience. Resilience to keep going, to move forward, to propel and to achieve. I was proving this to myself with my career, which was flourishing. I was financially independent and I was coping with all that was being thrown at me.

What I hadn't quite learnt yet was that resilience also needs reverence. I needed to respect why I had built up the resilience in the first place. I needed to respect pain, explore it, process it so as not to see it as a binary experience. I used to think: *It can take me down OR it can make me stronger.* I wasn't aware of the power of letting pain in until Matt's death. I realized that if I was to have any happiness in the future, if I was to have fulfilling and cherished relationships, and if I was to ever love and be loved again, then I was going to have to let the pain in. Let it flood me and overwhelm me and shake me so violently I thought it might break me.

Only then could I understand myself and all the choices I've made. Only then could I soften inside and let all the resilience I had built up inside me be powered by grace as well as fortitude. And I did, and I will continue to do, because it brings me great riches every day.

And as I sit here writing this book, dear reader, I am in love. For the first time since Matt died, I have met someone and fallen in love. Remember 'new man' from the BBQ? We met eleven days after I was offered this book deal and it was a random and unexpected meeting. His name is Ian and he is kind and funny and intelligent. The relationship has helped me understand the importance of all the work I have done before I met him. I can allow myself to be happy and in love without feeling any guilt. I can be vulnerable and scared and understand where it's coming from. I can be free and open, allowing myself to be seen without fear of abandonment.

We are in the very early stages of our relationship and even though I know the story will write itself, I sincerely hope it will be a long and exciting one. My experience of losing Dad and Matt means I can either live in dread that this new love will be taken away from me or I can cherish the time we do have together, knowing that life is precious. I choose the latter.

One of the things I was most scared of with a new relationship was him not being able to handle me talking about Matt. I needn't have worried. Ian has asked about Matt from the very beginning. About our time together, what he was like, what we did together. I have never once felt as though he sees him as a threat and it makes me have even more admiration for him. We talk freely about my dad too and Ian shares his losses with me. We have both reached an age where loss is inevitable in our lives and to share them is a great gift.

My relationship with my son has also strengthened as I've processed loss. He has watched me journey through grief, which has hopefully allowed him to face his own. He has had many losses for such a young man and I hope dearly that my honesty about my own pain helps him walk though his. He's a remarkable boy and I don't just say that because he's mine; I see it in the eyes of others who he speaks to. A few days ago he was off out with his friends for a meal. He's grown a lot recently so I offered him a shirt to wear that I thought might fit. It's an old vintage HUD jeans shirt of my dad's. I adore it and I thought Harvey might too.

'Ahh, cool,' he said. 'I like that.' And he put it on without a moment's hesitation. He looked great. Then he left in my dad's shirt while Ian and I had a night in together. Moments like that, which are difficult to imagine when you are in pain, feel so poignant. My little boy is wearing my dad's shirt and my new boyfriend is in my flat and all of it feels so natural.

Grief in childhood takes away your innocence, it gives you a wisdom and a stature that defies your years. I wouldn't wish it upon any child, but if we can hold them and walk them through it then when life inevitably doesn't go their way or they are faced with their first option B, then they remember: they have tools, they know where to go and what to do to help them through it. And, when they encounter another person going through a tough time, they have empathy and understanding, because they have been there too.

Today I feel stronger in my understanding of grief. I know it comes in waves; I can't control the strength of them, but if I accept it is coming I will judge myself less when they take me under. And they will. This idea of being a strong person only makes sense to me now if I am facing my grief. If I'm running (and you know how much I hate running), then it will only be a fleeting activity and grief will always win in the end anyway. So today I take the messy, slightly more uncomfortable route, and it suits me.

I try as much as I can to wear fewer masks. I want to be as honest as I can with people so I can connect with them, as I've discovered that connection is my lifeline. My work is more interesting because of it. The only thing actors are truly in control of is their point of view and how they approach a character and I feel confident in what I have to say now. The more I understand myself and what effects my experiences have had on me, the more confident I am embodying someone else's experience. I can use all my imagination AND my life experience because I've taken time to understand it. It may seem too weird to link this to my grief work but it's all about knowing myself and understanding the why behind everything. I can bring all of that knowledge into my work and it enriches my experience.

Christmas is only two weeks away as I write this. It's my first since losing Matt that I feel genuinely happy. Things have fallen into place since I moved back to the North-East. It's stopped feeling as though I'm swimming against the tide and yet my life looks so different to how I thought it would.

I imagined I would be in my house in London with Harvey and Matt and our new baby. I was going to live on the same street as Polly and we would be neighbours and forever having cups of tea in each other's houses. That was my option A, and it was taken.

Option B took me back home, to a place near the sea where I can walk to the water and talk to my loved ones as I watch the waves. It brought me back to my family, to the place that held so much love for me and so much pain. And because I wanted to walk this messy path, with all its discomfort and awkwardness, my family have come along on the journey too.

We got together this year to raise a glass on Dad's anniversary, we have a place to visit our brother Colin, we gathered at mine to remember Matt. I feel as though we have become more able to share our grief with each other. To celebrate our people as well as mourn them. Harvey is thriving and following his own dreams and I am in a relationship that I didn't think could exist after Matt. I have learnt that it is more than possible to love again. I've learnt that a reimagined life is not second best, but simply a new story.

Acknowledgements

To Mam. Thank you for everything you have given me and for your bravery and kindness. You are a true light in my life and I could not have travelled this road without you.

To Derek, my stepdad. Thank you for protecting us all and for giving us a safe and loving home. Thank you for the songs and the jokes and the stories of your days at sea. My dad would have been so proud of you.

To Nicola, Paula, Chelsea, Jess, Will, Penelope, Baxter, Pete and Ryan. Thank you for your love and kindness through all of this. I am so grateful.

To Polly. Thank you for your unending support and for pushing me to go on that retreat! I think I've used up all my superlatives about you in the book, but I hope you know just how much you mean to me.

To my girls in the North-East! We've known each other for so long and your friendship and encouragement mean the world to me. Thank you for being there for me.

To my agents, Kim and Roger. Thank you for your belief in me. Kim: thank you for asking me if I had any ideas for a book and for quite literally getting this whole thing going. You're amazing.

Morwenna, my literary agent. On the day we met, you sat and listened to me for hours, we ate biscuits, we laughed and cried a bit, and you never questioned what I was trying to convey. Thank you for believing in me.

To all at Pan Macmillan. Thank you for understanding the story I wanted to write and for giving me the opportunity to do so. I am forever grateful.

To Harvey. Thank you for being the most understanding and loving son. I adore you and you have given me so much strength without even knowing. I'm in awe of you and the way you handle everything.

To Ian. It's hard to express how happy I am that we have met. You have enriched my life and made me feel so completely loved. Your support and encouragement make me feel as though I could move mountains. Thank you.

To Donna. You gave me a chance to look at the world on a different axis and your friendship is so special to me. Thanks for the laughs and the stories.

To Zimms. Thank you for your kindness, your support, your understanding and the way you listened. Also, how honest you were about how you felt. God, I appreciated that so much! Thank you.

And to all my friends and family who reached out and sent words of kindness. There really are so many of you and you are all in my heart. I feel so very grateful to have you in my life.

Further reading

———

Bearing the Unbearable: Love, Loss and the Heartbreaking Path of Grief (Joanne Cacciatore)

Dark Nights of the Soul: A Guide to Finding Your Way Through Life's Ordeals (Thomas Moore)

In the Realm of Hungry Ghosts: Close Encounters with Addiction (Gabor Maté)

On Grief and Grieving: Finding the Meaning of Grief Through the Five Stages of Loss (Elisabeth Kubler-Ross and David Kessler)

Option B: Facing Adversity, Building Resilience and Finding Joy (Sheryl Sandberg and Adam Grant)

'TED Talk: The Power of Vulnerability' (Brené Brown)

The Bridge: A Nine-Step Crossing from Heartbreak to Wholehearted Living (Donna Lancaster)

When Things Fall Apart: Heart Advice for Difficult Times (Pema Chödrön)